Scrum - A Pocket Guide
4th edition

Other publications by Van Haren Publishing

Van Haren Publishing (VHP) specializes in titles on Best Practices, methods and standards within four domains:
- IT and IT Management
- Architecture (Enterprise and IT)
- Business Management and
- Project Management

Van Haren Publishing is also publishing on behalf of leading organizations and companies: BRMI, CA, Centre Henri Tudor, CATS CM, Gaming Works, IACCM, IAOP, IFDC, Innovation Value Institute, IPMA-NL, ITSqc, NAF, KNVI, PMI-NL, PON, The Open Group, The SOX Institute.

Topics are (per domain):

IT and IT Management	Enterprise Architecture	Business Management
ABC of ICT	ArchiMate®	*BABOK® Guide*
ASL®	GEA®	BIAN®
CMMI®	Novius Architectuur Methode	BiSL® and BiSL® Next
COBIT®	TOGAF®	BRMBOK™
e-CF		BTF
ISM	**Project Management**	CATS CM®
ISO/IEC 20000	A4-Projectmanagement	DID®
ISO/IEC 27001/27002	DSDM/Atern	EFQM
ISPL	ICB / NCB	eSCM
IT4IT®	ISO 21500	IACCM
IT-CMF™	MINCE®	ISA-95
IT Service CMM	M_o_R®	ISO 9000/9001
ITIL®	MSP®	OPBOK
MOF	P3O®	SixSigma
MSF	*PMBOK® Guide*	SOX
SABSA	Praxis®	SqEME®
SAF	PRINCE2®	
SIAM™		
TRIM		
VeriSM™		
XLA®		

For the latest information on VHP publications, visit our website: www.vanharen.net.

Scrum
A Pocket Guide
4th edition

A Smart Travel Companion

Colophon

Title:	Scrum - A Pocket Guide – 4th edition
Subtitle:	A Smart Travel Companion
Author:	Gunther Verheyen
Reviewers:	Ken Schwaber (Scrum co-creator, Scrum.org)
	David Starr (Agile Craftsman, Microsoft)
	Ralph Jocham (Agile Professional, effective agile.)
	Patricia M. Kong (Business Agility Enterprise Solutions, Scrum.org)
	Blake McMillan (Principal Consultant, Improving)
	Dominik Maximini (Agile Leadership Coach, ValueRise Consulting)
	Bhuvan Misra (Agile Mason)
Publisher:	Van Haren Publishing, 's-Hertogenbosch-NL
	www.vanharen.net
Lay-out and design:	Coco Bookmedia, Amersfoort-NL
ISBN Hard copy:	978 94 018 1221 4
ISBN eBook (pdf):	978 94 018 1222 1
ISBN ePub:	978 94 018 1223 8
Edition:	Fourth edition, first impression, August 2024
Copyright:	Gunther Verheyen & Van Haren Publishing

Although this publication has been composed with most care, neither author nor publisher can accept any liability for damage caused by possible errors and/or incompleteness in this publication.

No part of this publication may be reproduced in any form by print, photo print, microfilm or other means without written permission by the publisher.

Foreword by Ken Schwaber

An outstanding accomplishment that simmers with intelligence.

Scrum – A Pocket Guide is an extraordinarily competent book. Gunther has described everything about Scrum in well-formed, clearly written descriptions that flow with insight, understanding, and perception. Yet, you are never struck by these attributes. You simply benefit from them, later thinking, "That was really, really helpful. I found what I needed to know, readily understood what I wanted, and wasn't bothered by irrelevancies."

I have struggled to write this foreword. I feel the foreword should be as well-written as the book it describes. In this case, that is hard. Read Gunther's book. Read it in part, or read it in whole. You will be satisfied.

Scrum is simple, but complete and competent in addressing complex problems. Gunther's pocket guide is complete and competent in addressing understanding a simple framework for addressing complex problems, Scrum.

Ken, 22 August 2013

Preface

The use of lightweight, Agile methods continues to gain traction with Scrum being the most widely adopted framework. The general level of interest in Scrum is already huge and still its use keeps expanding, in and beyond software and (new) product development.

Transforming an organization's way of working to Scrum represents quite a challenge. Scrum is not a cookbook 'process' with detailed and exhaustive prescriptions for every imaginable situation. Scrum is a lightweight *framework* of principles, rules and values that thrives on the *people* employing Scrum. A major potential of Scrum is that it forms the stable foundation for the discovery and *emergence* of practices, tools and techniques and optimizing them for a specific context.

The benefits realized through Scrum depend on the will to remove barriers, think across walls and separations and embark on a journey of discovery.

That journey implies understanding the rules of Scrum to know how the game is played. Although there is ultimately nothing more powerful to learn Scrum than by going out and playing, this book also aspires to be your companion along the way, all the way. This book shows how Scrum implements the Agile mindset, what the rules of the game of Scrum are and how these rules leave room for a variety of tactics to play the game. The ambition of describing all these aspects is to make this book worthwhile for people, teams, managers and change agents regardless of whether they are already doing Scrum or want to embark on their journey of Scrum.

My own journey took off in 2003 with eXtreme Programming wrapped in Scrum and has inevitably been a cobblestone path. I have used Scrum with many teams, in various projects and initiatives, at different scales and at different organizations. I have worked with large and small enterprises and I have coached individual practitioners and teams as well as executive management. I have partnered with Ken Schwaber, co-creator of Scrum, while shepherding the 'Professional Scrum' trainings, courseware and assessments of Scrum.org. I am gratified that in 2016 I was able to continue my journey of humanizing the workplace with Scrum as an independent Scrum Caretaker.

In the meantime, evolving this book has turned into a journey in itself. I created the first edition in 2013. I remember how I described the Scrum Values in that first edition. In 2016 they were added to the Scrum Guide. In that first edition I also pointed out that the traditional three questions of the Daily Scrum are a good, but optional tactic. That optionality was added to the Scrum Guide in 2017 and the questions were not mentioned anymore in the 2020 edition, taking away all doubt that they are indeed optional.

However, more and bigger challenges keep surfacing. The balance of society keeps drastically and rapidly shifting from industrial (often physical) labor to digital (often virtual) work. In many domains of society, the unpredictability of work increases incessantly. The industrial paradigm is rendered useless, definitely, for many types of work. The need for the Agile paradigm is bigger than ever, and thus the need for a tangible framework like Scrum to help people and organizations increase their agility in performing complex work in complex circumstances.

Scrum is increasingly being discovered and appreciated as this *'empirical framework that enables people to derive value from complex challenges'*, more than as only a way to deliver (software) products. More and different people ask for guidance on their journey of Scrum, often in domains beyond software and new product development. It required a more generic description of the rules of Scrum, different words, other angles to the known set of rules. This is why I created the second edition of this book in 2019.

The focus of the third edition (2021) remained on clarifying the intent and purpose of the rules and roles in the framework, but it also introduced some changes in terminology. I learned from my readers that when Scrum is explained from its roots in software development it makes sense for people in other domains. I have learned from my readers that my book offers the, more than ever needed, foundational insights for people and their organizations to properly shape their Scrum, regardless of their domain or business.

Yet, as the 'doctrine of improvability' says: "There must be a better way."

My initial ambition with this fourth edition was to slightly improve the cohesion of my description of the rules of the game. This is reflected in my revised Scrum Game Board: all aspects of Scrum are now captured in that one visual (section 2.5). I obviously could not resist making some small updates and edits to what I wrote before, even to the parts I thought I would never touch again. It resulted in a complete update with much more refinements than originally anticipated and even a new section ("eXtreme Development", section 3.6). I am continuously uncovering better ways of explaining Scrum...

I thank Ken Schwaber for the foreword and his review for the original (2013) edition and all other reviewers for their much-appreciated feedback on the subsequent editions. I thank all translators for their past and on-going efforts to spread my words in different languages. I thank all at Van Haren Publishing, and especially Ivo van Haren, for allowing me to express my independent Scrum Caretaker view on Scrum.

Enjoy reading.

Gunther
independent Scrum Caretaker
June 2013, August 2018, November 2020, May 2024

Reviews

This Scrum Pocket Guide is outstanding. It is well organized, well written, and the content is excellent. This should be the de facto standard handout for all looking for a complete, yet clear overview of Scrum.

(Ken Schwaber, Scrum co-creator, August 2013)

Gunther has expertly packaged the right no-nonsense guidance for teams seeking agility, without a drop of hyperbole. This is the book about agility with Scrum I wish I had written.

(David Starr, Agile Craftsman, June 2013)

During my many Scrum training activities I often get asked: "For Scrum, what is the one book to read?" In the past the answer wasn't straightforward, but now it is! The Scrum Pocket Guide is the one book to read when starting with Scrum. It is a concise, yet complete and passionate reference about Scrum.

(Ralph Jocham, Agile Professional, June 2013)

"The house of Scrum is a warm house. It's a house where people are WELCOME." Gunther's passion for Scrum and its players is evident in his work and in each chapter of this book. He explains the Agile paradigm, lays out the Scrum framework and then discusses the 'future state of Scrum.' Intimately, in about 100 pages.

(Patricia M. Kong, Business Agility Enterprise Solutions, June 2013)

I recommend reading *Scrum – A Pocket Guide* early in your Scrum journey to help you gain a deeper understanding of why Scrum works and how the values and principles can positively impact the lives of your team as well as the health of an organization. Reading it later in your journey is great too… except for the feeling of regret wishing you had read it earlier.

(Blake McMillan, Principal Consultant, August 2018)

It is hard to find concise, to the point literature about Scrum. Most authors circle around the core topics instead of naming them. Gunther chose to break this pattern, enlightening us with the knowledge of the truly important parts of Scrum. When starting on your Scrum journey, make sure to take a copy of this guide along with you.

(Dominik Maximini, Agile Leadership Coach, August 2018)

"Small in size, big on value." Gunther's pocket guide to Scrum is one of the few books that I possess in both hardcopy and e-book format so that I have it with me all the time. It is a good read and a great companion to the Scrum Guide. Highly recommended for ambitious travelers!

(Bhuvan Misra, Agile Mason, November 2020)

Table of contents

1 THE AGILE PARADIGM 15
1.1 To Shift or not to Shift 15
1.2 The origins of Agile 20
1.3 Definition of Agile 21
1.4 The iterative-incremental continuum 25
1.5 Agility can't be planned 28
1.6 Combining Agile and Lean 31

2 SCRUM 39
2.1 The house of Scrum 39
2.2 Scrum, what's in a name? 40
2.3 Is that a gorilla I see over there? 43
2.4 Framework, not methodology 49
2.5 Playing the game 51
2.6 Core principles 66
2.7 The Scrum values 77

3 TACTICS FOR A PURPOSE 83
3.1 Visualizing progress 84
3.2 The Daily Scrum questions 86
3.3 Product Backlog refinement 87
3.4 User Stories 89

	3.5	Planning Poker	90
	3.6	eXtreme Development	91
	3.7	Sprint length	93
	3.8	Scrum in the Large	95

4 THE FUTURE STATE OF SCRUM 103

4.1	The power of the possible product	105
4.2	The upstream adoption of Scrum	108

ANNEXES

Annex A: Scrum Glossary 113
Annex B: Scrum Reference Card 119
Annex C: References 121

ABOUT THE AUTHOR 125

INDEX 129

1 The Agile Paradigm

■ 1.1 TO SHIFT OR NOT TO SHIFT

The software industry was for a long time dominated by a paradigm of *industrial* views and beliefs, based on and consisting of old manufacturing routines and theories. An essential element in this landscape of beliefs, views and practices was the Taylorist[1] conviction that 'workers' can't be trusted to intelligently, autonomously and creatively perform their work. Such 'workers' are expected to do no more than carry out pre-defined executable tasks. Their work must be prepared, designed and planned by more senior staff. And then still, hierarchical supervisors are expected to vigilantly oversee the execution of these carefully prepared tasks. *People are*

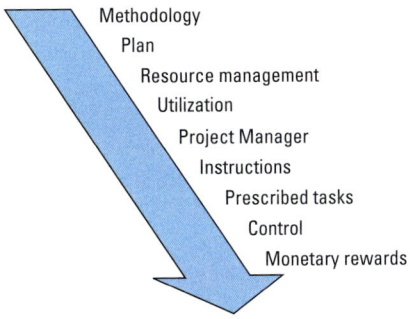

Figure 1.1 The Industrial Paradigm

treated as resources. Quality is assured by admitting the good and rejecting the bad batches of outputs. Monetary rewards and similar extrinsic motivators are used to stimulate desired behavior. Unwanted behavior is punished. *The old 'carrots and sticks' strategies.*

The serious flaws of the old paradigm in software development have been known and well documented for a long time. In particular, the Chaos reports of the Standish Group [Standish, 2011; Standish, 2013] have over and over revealed the low success rates of the traditional approach in software development. The shortcomings and errors resulting from the application of the industrial paradigm in software development are well beyond reasonable levels of tolerance. The unfortunate response was to lower the expectations. The definition of 'success' in the industrial paradigm is the combination of on time, within budget and including all predefined scope. It became accepted that only 10-20% of software projects were successful. *Although these success criteria can be disputed, it is the paradigm's promise.* It became accepted that quality is low and that over 50% of features of traditionally developed software applications are never used [Standish, 2002; Standish, 2013].

Although it is not widely and consciously admitted, the industrial paradigm did place the software industry in a serious crisis and gave it a bad reputation. Many tried to overcome this by fortifying the industrial approach even more. The exhaustiveness of upfront work was increased. More plans were created, more phases scheduled, more designs made, more control and other meetings planned, more signatures demanded, hoping that the actual execution would be done more effectively. As the success rates did not increase as a result of this fortification of the industrial paradigm, it was assumed that the instructions still were not clear and not detailed enough. And the core idea remained that the 'workers' needed to be directed. Even more detailed instructions were given. Supervision was increased and intensified. And so on. It is a vicious circle which did not lead to many improvements. The serious flaws, defects and low quality remained and had to be tolerated.

It took some time, but inevitably new ideas and insights started forming to finally overcome the significant anomalies of the industrial paradigm.

The seeds of a new world view were already sown in the 1990s. But it was in 2001 that these resulted in the formal naming of 'Agile', a turning-point in the history of work. A new paradigm was born, in the realm of the software industry. It is a paradigm that thrives upon heuristics and creativity, upon (restoring) the respect for the creative nature of the work and the intelligence of the 'workers'. In the meantime, it is expanding to many other domains of society.

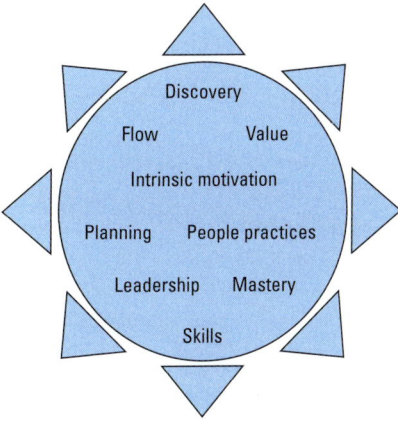

Figure 1.2 The Agile Paradigm

But even the software industry still has good reasons to keep embracing the new paradigm. The traditional flaws are significant and widely known while the presence of software in society grows exponentially, making it a critical aspect of our modern world. However, by definition, a shift to a new paradigm takes time. And the old paradigm seems to have deep roots and a considerable half-life time. An industrial approach to software development continues to be applied, taught and promoted as the most appropriate one, despite the clear flaws and failures.

Many say that Agile is too radical and they, therefore, propagate a gradual introduction of Agile practices within existing, traditional processes and procedures. However, there is reason to be very skeptical about such gradual evolution, a slow progression from the old to the new paradigm, from industrial to Agile.

The chances are high that such a gradual evolution will never go beyond the surface, will not do more than just scratch that surface. New names will be installed, new terms and new practices will be imposed, but the fundamental thinking and behaviors remain the same. Essential flaws remain untouched; especially the disrespect for people and the continued treatment of creative, intelligent people as mindless 'workers', as 'resources'.

The preservation of the traditional foundations also keeps existing data, metrics and standards in place, and the new paradigm will be measured against those old standards. Different paradigms by their nature, however, consist of fundamentally different and mutually exclusive concepts and ideas. No meaningful comparison between the industrial and the Agile paradigm is possible. No meaningful measurement of Agile against the old standards is possible.

It requires honesty to accept the serious flaws of the old ways. It requires leadership, vision, entrepreneurship and persistence to embrace the new ways, thereby abandoning and replacing the old thinking.

> A gradual shift to introduce the Agile paradigm results factually in a status quo situation that keeps the industrial paradigm intact.

There is overwhelming evidence that the old paradigm doesn't work for creative work like software development. Much of the evidence on the better results of Agile used to be anecdotal, personal or relatively minor. The Chaos report of 2011 by the Standish Group [Standish, 2011] marked a turning point. Extensive research was done in comparing traditional projects with projects that used Agile methods. The report shows that an Agile approach results in a much higher yield, even against the old expectations of delivery on time, on budget and with all the predefined scope. The report shows that Agile projects were three times more successful, and there were three times fewer failed Agile projects compared to traditional projects. These findings were confirmed in all later Chaos reports. For large projects the changes in success rates were less outspoken, which is likely more due to starting with the wrong expectations in the first place, i.e. the combination of time+budget+scope. Against the right expectations, with a focus on active customer collaboration and frequent delivery of value, the new paradigm would be performing even better, with frequent delivery of vertical slices of value to overcome the volume problem.

Yet, Agile is a choice, not a must. It is one way to improve. Research shows it is more successful.

Scrum helps.

Scrum is a tangible way to adopt and ingrain the Agile paradigm. The distinct rules of Scrum help in getting a grip on the new paradigm. The small set of prescriptions allows immediate action and results in a more fruitful, long-term absorption of the new, Agile paradigm. Using Scrum, people develop new ways of working; through discovery, experimentation-based learning and collaboration. They enter a new state of being, a state of *agility*. This process helps their organizations transform towards such a *state* of agility too, a state of constant change, flux, evolution and adaptation.

It allows freeing up time, people and energy for being innovative (again). Scrum becomes the bedrock of agility.

Nevertheless, despite its minimalism, experience shows that adopting Scrum often represents a giant leap. This may be because of the uncertainty induced by letting go of old certainties, even when those old certainties have proven not to be very reliable or…certain. It may be the time that it takes to make a substantial shift. It may be the determination and hard work that is required. Over and over again it is shown that Scrum is simple, not easy.

■ 1.2 THE ORIGINS OF AGILE

Despite the domination of the plan-driven, industrial views, an evolutionary approach to software development was not entirely new in 2001. Craig Larman has extensively described the historical predecessors of Agile in his book *'Agile & Iterative Development, A Manager's Guide'* [Larman, 2004].

But the official label 'Agile' dates from February 2001, when 17 software development leaders gathered at the Snowbird ski resort in Utah. They discussed their views on software development in times when failing heavy-weight, waterfall approaches were replaced by heavy-weight, waterfall-like RUP implementations ('Rational Unified Process'), which did not lead to better results. These development leaders were following different paths and methods, each being a distinct expression of what would become the new, Agile paradigm: Scrum, eXtreme Programming, Adaptive Software Development, Crystal, Feature Driven Development, etc.

After having considered calling them 'lightweight' first, the gathering resulted in assigning the label 'Agile' to the common principles, beliefs and thinking of these leaders and their methods. They were published as the *'Manifesto for Agile Software Development'* [Beck, et.al., 2001]. It turned into an expected success.

> We are uncovering better ways of developing
> software by doing it and helping others do it.
> Through this work we have come to value:
>
> **Individuals and interactions** over processes and tools
> **Working software** over comprehensive documentation
> **Customer collaboration** over contract negotiation
> **Responding to change** over following a plan
>
> That is, while there is value in the items on
> the right, we value the items on the left more.

Figure 1.3 The Agile Manifesto

The downside of that success is that the desire "to do Agile" or "to go Agile" is all too often the desire for a magical solution, another silver bullet approach that solves all problems. It makes me often state that *"Agile does not exist"*. This means that 'Agile' is not a fixed process, method or practice. It is the collection of principles that the methods for Agile software development have in common. It refers to the mindset, the convictions and the preferences expressed in the Manifesto for Agile Software Development.

When using the Manifesto as a source to gain a deeper understanding of Agile and the ideas underpinning it, I strongly advise looking at the twelve principles behind the four value statements (http://agilemanifesto.org/principles.html).

■ 1.3 DEFINITION OF AGILE

In the absence of a concise, specific definition I prefer describing 'Agile' in terms of three key characteristics. These are the traits that are common to the portfolio of Agile methods and are typical of an Agile way of working, regardless of the domain or industry:

- Collaborative people; *plus*
- Iterative-incremental progress; *plus*
- Value as the measure of success.

1.3.1 Collaboractive People

Agile is not a way of working driven by predictive plans on how to implement requirements that were exhaustively analyzed, designed, documented and architected in an upfront way and cannot be touched during the actual work. Agile acknowledges that how people use and what they need from a system (defined broadly) cannot be predicted in every possible detail in an upfront way.

Neither is Agile a process of handing over different types of intermediate deliverables to different types of specialists sequentially performing their specialized work in isolation.

Agile is driven by the continuous, *active collaboration* of *people*, of people upholding a 'collaboractive' stance throughout. Collaboractive people actively pursue collaborations across involved and required departments, whether they are known as business, IT, marketing, sales, HR, customer service, operations or management. Agile certainly does not know the traditional business versus IT discord. Both must be involved to successfully create products that are both usable *and* useful, products that are valuable.

The increased emphasis on collaboration, interaction and conversation calls for a different management style. Agile teams are *facilitated* and supported through servant-leadership. Minimally, boundaries and a context for self-management exist where teams are given objectives and direction, but are not being told how to do their work. Subtle control emerges from the boundaries, at the outset, not from controlling individuals, tasks or estimates. Collaboration and servant-leadership replace the traditional command-and-control mechanisms of instructing individuals on a daily basis with executable micro-tasks and of totalitarian authorities and invasive control.

People are respected for their creativity, intelligence and intrinsic self-organizing capabilities. People are respected for being able to perform the work for which they were hired. People are respected for their ability to understand and address a problem without being overloaded with tons of instructions, ceremony and bureaucracy. Ultimately, such a ceremonial overload only kills collaborative thinking, innovation and accountability of people anyhow, replacing it with and leaving only bureaucracy, paper results, handovers and administrative excuses.

People are respected in the time they can spend on their work via the idea of *Sustainable Pace*. Work is organized in such a way that the tempo is sustainable, indefinitely.

1.3.2 Iterative-Incremental Progress

Agile processes are not free-play approaches but require much *discipline*.

Products are created piece by piece ('incremental') where each piece is made up of expansions, improvements, eliminations and modifications to what was done before. The built pieces and the resulting total product are frequently revisited ('iterative') to assure the overall integrity.

Agile requires explicit attention from all players on quality and excellence. Agile replaces the idea that these can be poured into documents and paper descriptions that have very different properties than the envisioned final result, i.e. the releasable product or service.

The need for an iterative-incremental process is augmented by the finding that requirements and implementation are prone to change, no matter how much time, energy and funding are spent on predicting and planning them in an upfront way. The evolution of markets and competitors, users only knowing what they want when they get to use it and changes to enterprise strategies are but a few of the changes that will have an impact. Contrary to a predictive process, change is not excluded from nor expelled to the ceremonial outskirts of development. Agile calls for an extreme awareness and openness for change.

New insights, evolving opinions and changed priorities even form the living heart of an Agile system. Agile thrives upon such *emergence* and subsequent gradual evolution of requirements, plans, ideas, architectures and designs. Change is not disruptive because it forms a natural part of the regular way of working.

In my view, Agile should even *encourage* change as a source of innovation and improvement through acts of deliberate emergence, not just expecting events to happen but deliberately provoking them, knowing that risk is mitigated by working in short cycles and the iterative-incremental process.

1.3.3 Value as the Measure of Success

Success in environments that thrive on emergence cannot be measured and guaranteed on the basis of mere compliance with predictive plans and milestones, documents, handovers, signatures, approvals or other ceremonial obligations; as is the case in the industrial paradigm. Agile introduces new ways of measuring progress and success.

Agile makes explicit that progress and success can only be determined by frequently inspecting *working versions* of product and the actual *value* that they bring. To guarantee learning, it is imperative that the inspected work has all the characteristics of the final product. Intermediate descriptions of it, paper reports or presentations do not meet that demand.

It is a natural part of product development that the people having to use the product can only assess its usability and usefulness when they actually get their hands on it. No paper documentation or virtual process can replace this. It is an invitation to use an iterative-incremental development process and to close the feedback loop with users regularly to capture our impact and their appreciation. That is a crucial source of information for further evolutions of the product.

> Product is the vehicle to deliver value.

1.4 THE ITERATIVE-INCREMENTAL CONTINUUM

An Agile approach slices time into time-boxed iterations, periods having a fixed start and end date.

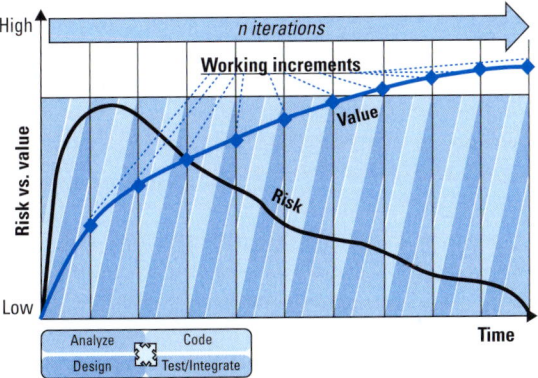

Figure 1.4 Agile Value Delivery

There are many advantages to this technique of time-boxing. *Focus* is certainly a very important one. Time-boxing also allows the absorption of pivots or disruptive changes, while ensuring regular checks so that lessons learned can be incorporated from one iteration to the next, even in a situation of more continuous flow. The core objective of each iteration is to create versions of valuable, working versions of product in order to gather feedback and enable early learning.

In Agile all development work is reorganized to optimize the ability to respond to and capitalize on *business* opportunities.

'Value' is the answer to user, market and business demands and the overall measure of progress and success. Value is an internal assumption within the organization until the work is actually released to the marketplace. Releasing product versions to the marketplace is the only way to validate the assumption of value. Releasing to the marketplace regularly is the only way to gather and incorporate the feedback and appreciation, or lack thereof, from the marketplace. This information is crucial for subsequent evolutions of the product. Work is continuously optimized for value. Value is continuously optimized across iterations.

Risk is controlled by consecutively producing working increments based upon defined development standards. 'Risk' therefore also relates to the *business* perspective of the work. Bear in mind that, certainly in an IT context, risk is typically defined as something technical (*Will the system perform? Is the system scalable?*). This, however, only covers the aspect of a product being *usable* (*Will it technically hold? Not break?*). But such a merely technical perspective on risk ignores the fact that the ultimate goal of Agile development is to provide greater satisfaction with end-users and customers, to ensure that the product is *useful*. A product being *usable*, from a technical perspective on risk, is just the beginning. Products need to be both usable *and* useful to be successful in the sense of delivering value.

Any modern development process should address the risk of not being able to capitalize on unforeseen and previously unknown *market* opportunities, the risk of not releasing product fast enough, the risk of customer dissatisfaction by releasing untested work or functions that are not what users expect or appreciate, the risk of lagging behind with regards to the competition.

Agile development is organized in a way that maximally mitigates those business risks. High-value needs are answered first. Product versions and updates are released quickly and frequently. They satisfy existing needs while also offering unexpected, innovative functions. They get users to pay for the product and optimize the stakeholders' return. They are of high quality in order to not decrease user satisfaction, but also to minimize maintenance and support, thus optimizing the *Total Cost of Ownership* ('TCO'). Agile development is organized in such a way that the people doing the core work start engaging (again) and derive value from adopting the Agile paradigm in that sense.

Agile software development breaks up the sequential organization of the 'normal' IT activities (in figure 1.4 coarsely represented as 'Analyze', 'Design', 'Code' and 'Test/Integrate'). To produce releasable versions of product, these activities are performed in a non-linear, incremental way, concurrently and on a daily basis by cross-skilled teams with continuous, active collaboration and negotiation about emergent ideas, techniques and practices. The goal is to enable flexibility, dynamism, business benefits and speed, instead of blocking them.

The goal of such an integrated, cross-functional approach is to build-in quality and to prevent defects, rather than attempt to establish quality by a bug-hunting approach in a post-creation phase. Quality cannot be added to a finished product. Delays and budgets grow well out of hand when a lack of quality is identified after the actual creation process is over.

Aiming at the real and lasting benefits of Agile development requires going beyond the borders of the IT (or similarly technical) departments. The way that Agile not only embraces and incorporates change but should even encourage it, is likely to challenge large parts of an organization. Rather than being an annoyance, this represents an *opportunity*. An entire organization will prosper from adopting an Agile way of working with its short cycles, frequent results and evolutionary adaptations. The Agile views and approach allow larger parts of organizations and its departments to finally stop trying to predict the unpredictable. Agile thrives on dealing with answers, solutions and competing ideas that emerge *while* delivering product.

It might take some time to experience the fact that the continuous learning innate in Agile actually increases the level of control in turbulent enterprise, business and market circumstances. It might take some time to shift management focus away from continuously making judgments over the past, like is done through actuals and time registrations, towards building on the impact and outcomes of the output and the work performed. It might take some time to gain confidence in the Agile development process and optimizing for value through feedback from its incrementally produced outcomes.

It might take some time to accept that agility takes time. It might take some time to accept that agility need not be analyzed, designed and planned upfront.

■ 1.5   AGILITY CAN'T BE PLANNED

Agility is the *state* envisioned by moving to an Agile way of working. Agility is a state of continuous flux, high responsiveness, speed and adaptiveness. It is a state needed to deal with the unpredictability so common to creative work, like software and other forms of new product development, and to the moving markets that organizations operate within.

Agility has no purpose if the aforementioned characteristics of flux, responsiveness, speed and adaptiveness are not expanded to the relationship of the team with the surrounding organization and to the relationship of the organization and its markets, user communities and consumers. The adoption of Agile processes, like Scrum, is an important foundation for such *enterprise* agility. From that adoption, new ways of working, interacting and collaborating emerge, together with a new organizational culture of learning, improving, adaptation and restored respect for people.

Throughout such an adoption important learnings are ingrained and injected into an organization's DNA.

There are some basic truths that are fundamental to any transformation toward a state of increased agility. When these essential truths are ignored, the door to increased agility is closed rather than becoming a gateway of opportunities:

- Agility can't be planned;
- Agility can't be dictated;
- Agility can't be copied;
- Agility has no end-state.

A time-planned way to become (more) Agile introduces awkward and unfavorable expectations. Agile is a new paradigm and the shift toward it will cause significant organizational turmoil. Existing procedures, departments and functions are impacted. Organizational constructs are questioned. Such change is highly complex and unpredictable. There is no way of predicting what needs will be encountered at what point in time, how these will have to be dealt with, how the new ways of working are being ingrained and what the exact outcome will be in order to plan and control the next steps. There is no way of predicting the pace at which the change will spread and take root.

Agility requires much more than following a new process. It is about behavior and in that sense about *cultural* change. A decision to move to Agile is a decision to leave the old (industrial) ways behind. It is not only about accepting but even more about celebrating and living the art of the possible. It requires the courage, honesty and determination of acting in the moment, acting upon the reality that is exposed by iterative-incremental progress information. Agility is about doing the best possible at every possible moment, constrained by the means we have and other constraints that surface. A time-planned way ignores the essence of Agile, that of dealing with complexity via well-considered steps of experimentation and learning. Time-planning for agility simply extends the old thinking. It is even counterproductive as a traditional plan will actually slow down the transformation process because it introduces delays, handovers and waiting times.

Time-plans also create the illusion of deadlines and a final end-state. Yet, agility has no end-state. Agility is a state of continuous improvement, a state in which each status quo is challenged, by our own will or by external turbulence, if not today then tomorrow.

Agility is a unique and continuously evolving state that holds and reflects the lessons and learnings that an organization went and goes through, the way in which specific annoyances and hindrances were and are overcome, the many inspections and adaptations that inevitably occur along the journey. Agility is a unique signature, with imprints of the people, relationships, interactions, tools, processes, practices and constructs within and across the many ecosystems that exist in and adjacent to an organization. No model or blueprint can predict, outline or capture such a unique signature. Agility is a path requiring vision, belief, persistence and . . . hard work.

Agility is a state of high adaptability that is achieved by regularly inspecting and adapting upon observable work results. What works today might not work tomorrow. What works for one combination of teams, technology and business might not work for another combination. Inspection without adaptation is pointless in a world of complexity, creativity, fierce competition and unpredictability. Adaptation without vision, observation and inspection on the other hand is ungrounded and directionless.

Living the art of the possible against inexactly predictable results is a call for people to engage. It motivates, since all players co-shape the future, thriving upon the unwritten state of that future and what that future might bring. Accepting the unwritten nature of the future can thus accelerate a transformation. It is a bright future for organizations that have the vision, the determination and the dedication, for organizations that have the courage to move away from following a plan or copying a model.

These basic truths must be in the hearts and minds of every person managing, guiding, facilitating, living or leading a transformation towards a more Agile way of working. And even then, it still takes time for agility to settle in the hearts and minds of the people impacted. After all, people have been instructed in 'wrong' behavior through the industrial paradigm for several decades.

> Scrum is a foundation, the bedrock for agility.

■ 1.6 COMBINING AGILE AND LEAN

It is vital to be aware that Lean, much like Agile, offers a set of thinking tools, a collection of interwoven principles that educate, motivate, value and guide people to continuously optimize their work and the way in which they undertake this work. The principles of Lean form the levers of a system that people can use to manufacture better products faster, yet in a sustainable and respectful way.

There is not one definitive, full-blown, one-size-fits-all, unified Lean process with predefined and prescribed phases, roles, definitions, artifacts, deliverables, etc. for product development or for manufacturing. A Lean process should be designed upon the underlying principles and thinking and be constantly tuned to the actual situation. It's about adaptiveness. *The online 'Lean Primer' document of Bas Vodde and Craig Larman [Larman & Vodde, 2009] does an excellent job of introducing the roots of Lean along with its principles and thinking.*

1.6.1 Major Aspects of Lean

People

The cornerstone of any system that claims to be Lean are the *people*. And 'people' refers to every possible actor in the whole ecosystem of a Lean product development/build system: customers, workers, teams, suppliers and managers; both internal and external.

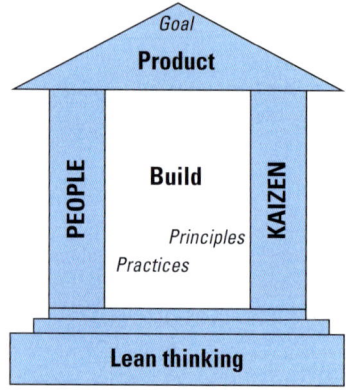

Figure 1.5 The Temple of Lean

All people contribute in their own way and by their own means to manufacturing a product. They collaborate to avoid handovers, delays and waiting times. They autonomously take decisions. They take the room to focus on knowledge gathering and constant learning. Managers act as teachers with a *go-see* commitment of work floor presence. They promote the Lean thinking system by helping people understand how to reflect on their work, their work results and how to build better products. The whole system embodies the spirit of *Kaizen*, the attitude of continuously thinking about the process, the product and possible improvements. Each member in the system can '*stop the line*'[2] if a problem occurs. The root of the problem needs to be identified in order for countermeasures to be proposed and installed.

Everyone involved in the value chain works in an integrated way. Relationships with suppliers and external partners are not based upon the traditional approach of large volume purchases, big negotiation rounds and pressuring one another. It's all about building relationships on the mutual sharing of profit (and risk). Lean partnerships are about mutual growth.

Waste

When considering the subject of waste, it is important that *avoiding* waste, via continuous improvement and small step optimizations, is the preferred option. Furthermore, 'waste' refers to process steps, not to people (as an excuse to get rid of people).

Obviously, no matter how much attention is paid to avoiding it, waste can and will creep in. The Kaizen spirit drives all people to be committed, aware and critical in their daily work. It's a natural reflex to detect waste and initiate actions to remove and prevent it.

A practice to identify structural waste is *Value Stream Mapping*. All steps and phases in the process of going from 'idea' to 'cash' are set out on a timeline. Activities may be labeled as 'valuable' or as 'non-value adding', but possibly also as necessary although not directly value-adding. The *Value Ratio* can be calculated as the ratio of time spent on value-adding activities versus wasteful activities. It's a figure that may serve as a baseline against which improvement can be measured. But, as in all improvement activities, there is no definite end goal, no final state. The improvement itself is the goal.

Inventory, WIP and Flow

Lean strives for continuity and flow. Overproduction and excessive inventory disrupt flow and may delay the discovery and resolution of quality issues. But it is also disrespectful as it forces people to do work that may actually never be used. Inventory is costly and makes an organization liable to incur losses.

Lean says to limit 'Work in Process' (and costly inventory) by producing only materials to be used further down the line in a 'Just in Time' mode, i.e. when there is a *pull* signal from the next steps in the process. A *kanban* is a physical signal card for this function in manufacturing systems. A kanban is attached to an inventory of parts. It is linked to a level of inventory. New parts are only produced when enough materials have been used and the signal card appears.

1.6.2 Implementing Lean

Much like with Agile, many organizations struggle with Lean. And on top of that, organizations struggle with the combination of Agile and Lean.

In general, companies refer to managerial or organizational problems when expressing a desire for 'Lean'. If they want to do 'Agile' on the other hand, they are most likely referring to problems with product development. However, neither Agile nor Lean offer one magical, off-the-shelf (silver bullet) solution.

Unfortunately, Lean is far too often limited to *eliminate waste*. Just picking out that one element from the toolbox is already an undesirable over-focus on just one aspect, instead of looking at the whole. It gets even worse when the principle itself is broken and 'elimination' is applied to (getting rid of) *people* and not as a means to improve *processes* and *structures*. The highly popular management sport of 'cost cutting' tends to twist this important Lean practice into designating people's work as 'overhead', i.e. non-valuable. The underlying signal is that the people who are doing that work are waste and . . . disposable.

It can be a long journey to move on from this popular misconception and all too limited perspective on Lean, and build up an understanding that Lean is primarily about respecting people in order to optimize value and quality. That Lean is more about the *context* in which people can prosper in order to perform than about continuously over-stressing the need for results and performance. It invokes the difficult exercise of replacing 'command and control', big boss behavior, micro-management, over-allocation and nano-assignments with decentralized decision-making mechanisms.

It is a long way from this misconception through to an understanding of Lean beyond the formal practices, an understanding of Lean as a thinking context with no definite end-state, with people continuously reflecting on their daily work and self-improving.

Agile helps.

There are more than just a few similarities between Agile and Lean that are worthwhile exploring. Some management or governance philosophies should not be mixed because it results in a blurry amalgam with the unique flavor of the ingredients as well as the benefits getting lost in the mix. But, as far as Agile and Lean are concerned, I not only believe that Lean and Agile *can* be combined; the combination, as a total outcome, will actually result in a more powerful mix.

Lean and Agile are truly *blending* philosophies. Lean thrives on a powerful but typical mindset. Agile has distinct views that not only match the main Lean principles extremely well, but even form a very tangible implementation of them for product delivery purposes.

1.6.3 The Blending Philosophies of Lean and Agile

'*The Blending Philosophies of Lean and Agile*' is also the title of a more detailed paper I have published on this subject [Verheyen, 2011]. Here I introduce just some of the clear strategies in Agile that align it with Lean:

- *Potentially unused inventories*: Detailed requirements, hard-coded plans, designs, etc. form a liability in software development and other forms of complex work, and not an asset, because they represent potentially unused work. Agile avoids producing these upfront in every possible detail and replaces them with emergence and just-in-time work. If the potential point of implementation of identified work is still some time away, the chances are considerable that the work will not have to be performed. And even if it is performed, the exact expectations may have changed in the meantime, or experience from intermediate implementation and releases may have revealed better ways of doing that future work. Only the upcoming, highest ordered work is detailed more, as this is what will be worked on next. And even then, a team will only *pull* in the amount of work they deem feasible for an iteration and start building it based on progressive learning and continuous improvement, even on a daily basis.

- *Partially done work*: Work that is not completely finished, 'almost there, I just need a little more time'-type of work, is a known, important type of waste. In an Agile process the goal of each iteration is to produce a *working* piece of product. No unfinished work is included in the observable result. Time-boxing is a time-management technique that helps teams focus on finishing work, as does limiting WIP ('Work in Process').

- *Feature usage*: Research has shown that barely 20% of the features included in a (software) product built in a traditional way are regularly used [Standish, 2002; Standish 2013]. Unused or under-used functions thus represent an enormous waste of effort and budget, both in terms of developing as well as maintaining them. Active collaboration with people who know and represent the customers and users prevents the production of unwanted or non-valuable requirements and helps a team focus on minimal sets of features that may actually be appreciated. The focus on 'wanted' requirements saves not only development budget. It also ensures that future maintenance and support costs can be kept much lower. And the iterative-incremental process allows for regularly adapting the product based on observations of the effective appreciation, or lack thereof, of the delivered work and capitalizing on new value opportunities.

Agile has clear strategies for continuous improvement, thereby leveraging the Kaizen spirit:
- The work plan of an Agile team is checked and updated daily;
- At the end of an iteration the product version (whether released or in a state of being releasable) is verified to gather feedback, remarks, improvements and enhancements;
- The process, the way the teams work, collaborate, communicate and undertake implementation, is regularly verified via retrospectives.

Agile *optimizes the whole* by demanding that customers or their proxies express and order work and take an active part in the implementation and development process for clarification and functional trade-offs. All skills are available within a team to turn ideas, options and requirements into working versions in a single iteration.

Agile shortens cycle times by optimizing the value stream through the prevention of traditional waiting activities like handovers and external decisions. There are no macro handovers, i.e. handovers across departments and organizations, which typically occur in a sequential organization of work with large blocks of specialized work packages. But there are also no micro handovers, i.e. handovers between individuals within a team, given the collective accountability of the team.

In general, the strategies and principles of Agile are consistent with, and even leverage, all major Lean principles, as indicated in the following representation:

Lean	Agile
Respect for people	Self-organizing teams
Kaizen	Inspect & adapt, short feedback cycles
Prevent/eliminate waste	No unused specs, architecture or infrastructure
Pull inventory (Kanban)	Estimates and planned work reflect actual capacity
Visual management	Information radiators
Built-in quality	Definition of Done, Development standards
Customer value	Active business collaboration
Optimizing the whole	Whole team together (incl. stakeholders)
Deliver fast	Time-boxed iterations and working Increments
The manager-teacher	The facilitating servant-leader

Figure 1.6 The Consistency in Principles of Lean and Agile

---

1 Frederick Taylor (1856-1915) was an American engineer who is best known for his research into ways to maximize the productivity and efficiency of labor while minimizing its cost. He promoted enforced standardization and the enforced adoption of systematic methods and practices. Control lay exclusively with management, with workers being there only to carry out the work.
2 This refers to the Toyota car manufacturing origins of Lean (TPS, Toyota Production System), where every person at the production line is entitled to stop the line when problems, defects or a lack of quality are detected.

2 Scrum

■ 2.1 THE HOUSE OF SCRUM

The house of Scrum is a warm house. It's a house where people are
W E L C O M E.

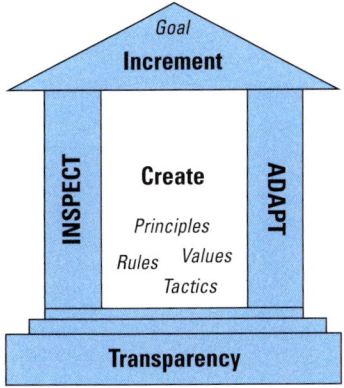

Figure 2.1 The House of Scrum

In the house of Scrum people from different backgrounds, in different roles, with different skills, talents and personalities work, learn and improve together. The house of Scrum is an inclusive house of warm, open and collaborative relationships.

The house of Scrum knows no 'versus'. Barriers are removed, instead of being maintained or created. There's no business versus IT in the house of Scrum, no team versus the organization, no Product Owner versus stakeholders, no coding versus supporting, no testers versus programmers, no 'my' team versus 'your' team, no Scrum Master versus managers. The house of Scrum offers an open view on the world. It is a great and energizing place where product development prospers from the combined, creative intelligence of self-developing people.

The house of Scrum helps to stay away from rigid behavior and structures, as rigidity is antithetical to agility. The inhabitants of the house of Scrum, their teams and the ecosystems in which they operate show flexibility in dealing with uncertainty and internal tensions within, and external pressure on, the ecosystem. They probe, sense and adapt at all levels: strategies, tactics, ideas, plans, objectives, markets, technology.

In the house of Scrum, energy and work pleasure are restored for all involved players and actors. This is how Scrum enables the creation and delivery of better products and services, faster. Scrum enables generating value for those who create the products and services, for those who sponsor the work and have a stakeholder interest in it, for those who consume the products and services, for all those who co-create them with opinions, feedback and appreciation. The workplace is humanized upon Scrum to restore the engagement of its inhabitants. Because engaged people actually care a lot more (about team, customer and enterprise outcomes). They need not be told to do so.

■ 2.2 SCRUM, WHAT'S IN A NAME?

The term 'Scrum' was first used by Hirotaka Takeuchi and Ikujiro Nonaka in their ground-breaking 1986 paper '*The New New Product Development Game*' [Takeuchi & Nonaka, 1986].

Their research, described in that paper, showed that outstanding performance in the development of new, complex products is achieved by *self-organizing teams*. They described how performance is most optimal when such multi-disciplinary units of people are given direction (not tasks) and are then expected to devise their own tactics on how to best achieve the joint objectives. Teams require autonomy to achieve excellence.

If teams are only instructed to carry out executable tasks and their capacity in hours is pre-filled with such tasks, team members suffer from a narrowed mind. They are restricted from looking and thinking beyond the instructions, even if reality or experience shows that the prescribed solution is difficult to achieve or is suboptimal. They lose openness for better solutions, solutions that are not dictated but are a better answer to the actual demand and objectives given changes, proven findings and current circumstances. Their only focus is to produce what was instructed without considering conflicting ideas and options, without dealing with this natural instability typical of product development and technological discovery. The industrial mode to direct people as if they are robots impedes capitalizing on the collective intelligence of a team, thereby limiting upfront their work results to mediocre levels.

The role of management is to act as an investor by not intervening on a daily basis but instead providing guidance, funding and moral support from the outset. With the term 'Scrum' the authors referred to the game of rugby to stress the importance of teamwork in achieving success in the 'game' of new product development.

Peter DeGrace and Leslie Hulet Stahl pointed out the potential value of applying the described principles of self-organization in software development, with the idea to call that "Scrum" [DeGrace & Stahl, 1990]. In the early 1990s, Jeff Sutherland and Ken Schwaber drove forward the development of an actual, tangible development process. They added empirical process control to the principle of self-organization in the

> ... as in Rugby, the ball gets passed within the team as it moves as a unit up the field.
> Takeuchi & Nonaka (1986).
> *The New New Product Development Game*

Figure 2.2 A Scrum in the Game of Rugby

framework that they presented as "Scrum" in 1995 at the OOPSLA conference ("Object-Oriented Programming, Systems, Languages & Applications") in Austin, Texas (US) [Schwaber, 1995; Sutherland, 1995]. The Scrum framework for developing and sustaining complex products as we know it today was mostly shaped in the years that followed through their collaboration with a group of patterns people [Beedle, et.al., 1998]. In my paper '*Scrum: A Brief History of a Long-Lived Hype*' I have documented not just these historical roots of Scrum but all the important steps and evolutions to date [Verheyen, 2023].

The remarkable similarities between Lean and Agile were pointed out in section 1.6. There is also a connection between Scrum and Lean via '*The New New Product Development Game*'.

Takeuchi and Nonaka are very familiar with, and are proponents of, Lean. Over the course of their careers and assignments they have studied and described well-known Lean companies. Yet, they never use the term 'Lean'.

In their paper, they chose to describe the beating heart of Lean, 'Scrum', as the differentiator in complex product development. Their message is that an organization is unlikely to benefit from any so-called 'Lean' practices if this beating heart (Scrum) is not present and only the surrounding practices are installed. Because this is the case for many Lean implementations, the authors preferred to stress the need for the heart and soul of the system and take away the focus on the surrounding management practices.

So, they opted not to mention Lean and focus instead on its essential engine, Scrum. They barely talk about 'Lean' because it became synonymous with just the *management* practices of the Toyota Production System.

> "Scrum should be at the heart of every implementation of Lean." [Sutherland, 2011]

■ 2.3   IS THAT A GORILLA I SEE OVER THERE?

Evolutionary practices for software and new product development have been around for a long time [Larman, 2004]. The Scrum process for software development was shaped throughout the 1990s and has kept its simplicity to date [Verheyen, 2023]. The Agile movement took off in 2001 [Beck, et.al., 2001]. This new paradigm quickly took root and its adoption via Scrum has been increasing steadily, also beyond software development where it originates from.

A widely accepted model to assess and represent the degree of adoption of a technological product or service is Geoffrey Moore's 'Technology Adoption Life Cycle' (TALC) [Moore, 1999; Wiefels, 2002].

Geoffrey Moore based his specific variant on the difference observed in the adoption pattern for *technology* products or services representing an important *disruptive* discontinuity. Moore confirmed that the general adoption phases and audiences of such products are in line with those of traditional products that are part of a more continuous evolution. But Moore observed and added a period of stagnation after the phase of *Early Market*. It is a period where adoption stalls. An unpredictable time passes by before entering the next phase of adoption, the *Bowling Alley*. Moore called this period the *Chasm*. Some products never even get out of this stand-still and simply disappear.

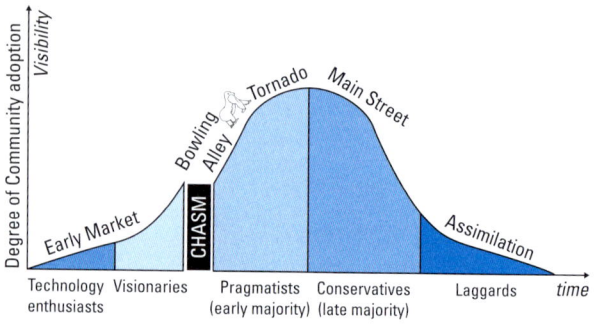

Figure 2.3 The Technology Adoption Life Cycle

During the highly turbulent phase of the Bowling Alley a *gorilla* is formed, a market leader. Until the product disappears from the market, gorilla-market leaders are difficult to overthrow.

During the *Tornado* phase, the adoption and dominance of the now must-have product keeps increasing. But it is only a highly creative phase that ignites even more innovation for those willing to head the herd, for those that allow the new, must-have product to drive forward the emergence of fundamentally new infrastructure, businesses and organizations, potentially causing even complete swap-outs of them.

In addition to the use of Agile for the delivery of new, possibly disruptive, products and services, Agile is a new, disruptive paradigm in itself. Moore's TALC is a tool to observe the adoption of Agile.

Around 2007 Agile was crossing the Chasm. Up to that point, evidence on Agile was mostly anecdotal and generally based on individual enterprise adoptions, isolated cases and personal storytelling. This is typical for these

early phases of the adoption life cycle. It is equally typical that mostly
enthusiasts and visionaries were attracted by it. But once Agile crossed
the Chasm, it also became attractive to a broader audience, the audience
of early majority-Pragmatists. They typically look at the business or
competitive advantages of a less proven paradigm and compare its problem-
solving capabilities to the existing paradigm for the decision to adopt it, or
not.

Important evolutions and revolutions in the world of technology, online
and digital in 2007-2008 certainly boosted the need for a new approach
to software and software development [Highsmith, 2023]. This definitive
breakthrough of the Internet era sparked the interest in and likely caused
the steep advent of Agile methods, helping the paradigm to cross the
Chasm. Yahoo! is an important example of a large company transitioning to
Agile in those years and documenting their experiences [Benefield, 2008].

In Q3 2009, Forrester Research and Dr. Dobb's [Hammond & West,
2009] conducted a survey amongst IT professionals worldwide including
inquiring about the type of "methodology (that) most closely reflects the
development process you are currently using". Perhaps surprisingly, 36%
of the participants indicated that they were doing Agile, while only 13%
confirmed to be following a waterfall process. 31% of the respondents
indicated not to be following any methodology and 21% indicated they were
doing iterative development. This confirmed the common perception that
Agile had indeed gradually been overtaking the waterfall model and that
Agile had crossed the Chasm.

In April 2012, Forrester Research [Giudice, 2011] published the results
of a survey on the global adoption of Agile for software application
development. They noted that "the IT industry is (...) widely adopting
Agile" and that the adoption of Agile was not limited to small enterprises
anymore. Large enterprises started forming a substantial part of the
companies moving to Agile. Forrester also found that "Shorter iterations

and Scrum practices are the most common Agile practices" and confirmed the widespread finding that Scrum had become the most applied method for Agile software development. Forrester thereby validated the results of the yearly *State of Agile Development* surveys conducted by VersionOne [VersionOne, 2011; VersionOne, 2013].

Although the adoption of Scrum is not typical of, or limited to, a specific economic sector, Forrester found that the financial services industry showed a remarkably high adoption rate of Agile methods. This is striking as large financial institutions are by their nature very risk averse. In the aftermath of the global financial crisis of 2008, it seems that many began adopting Scrum to ensure their future competitiveness, as I documented for a large financial organization headquartered in the Netherlands in 2012 [Verheyen & Arooni, 2012].

The post-Chasm years of Agile show many back-and-forth movements. These post-Chasm years of Agile are marked by a strong whirlwind with Scrum as an anchor and reference.

Inside of this whirlwind, three waves of Scrum have manifested so far:
- The first wave of Scrum was mostly a reconnaissance wave. Organizations found that the old, industrial ways no longer sufficed to solve, or even patch up, the problems in their IT and software delivery, certainly in the era of online and digital. Scrum was typically adopted as the new IT delivery process.
- During the second wave of Scrum, large organizations acknowledged they were at the end of the old ways of working too. Their leadership typically looked for ways to fit some derivative of Scrum into their existing, large organizational structures and thus 'scale' it. While Scrum's terminology was everywhere, sub-groups and derivative methods and movements trying to capitalize on this need took off. New names, movements and methods were invented, introduced, launched,

and often disbanded again. As Scrum entered this new market segment, divergence and 'scale' became the dominant themes.
- In the third Scrum Wave, organizations adopted Scrum, or some derivative, as the focal point of so-called 'Agile transformations'. These efforts were typically limited to building Agile teams only upon traditional, industrial thinking patterns. The result was rarely more than an *illusion of agility*. Often after a few years of investing, the *deflation by reality* hit hard when organizations found that their actual increase in agility was not what they hoped it would be [Verheyen, 2022]. A vast majority of such transformation efforts plainly failed. More Agile teams does indeed not make a more Agile organization.

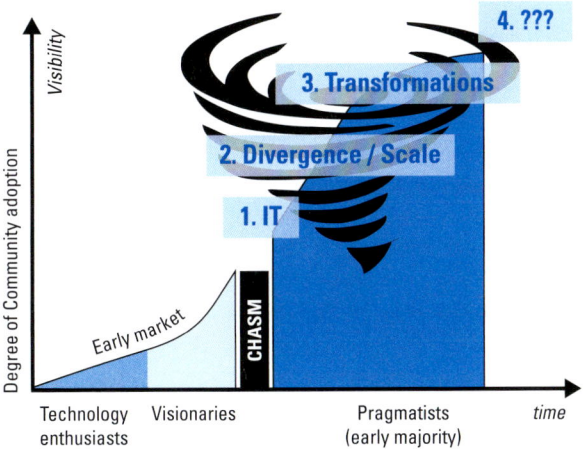

Figure 2.4 The Core Themes of the Scrum Waves

What the future following these three Scrum Waves brings is unsure. The whirlwind might start calming down. It could also change position or direction. Or it might circle towards areas unknown. Regardless, as even more organizations in even more domains of society continue to start using Scrum, its dominant gorilla position in Agile post-Chasm is confirmed.

Rather than remaining in the third Scrum Wave, I believe we are entering a fourth Scrum Wave. What its predominant themes will be remains unsure. After all, while we can remember the past, we cannot remember the future. However, we can shape the future.

Shaping the future of Scrum will certainly require courageous practitioners who, regardless of their role, function or position, will need to step up and help their organizations and leadership overcome the stagnation following the disappointments over the many failed Agile transformations and the complacency connected to the mass adoption of Scrum. The message to leadership that Scrum is a well-defined and clearly stated, yet highly flexible solution (because the rules leave much room for various tactics) is still a valid message. There is no need for management to impose the same one way of Scrum on every team throughout an organization. It is possible to standardize on Scrum without industrializing it to death.

I also believe that entering the fourth Scrum Wave coincides with transitioning into the Tornado phase of the Technology Adoption Life Cycle of Agile. It means that Scrum will be used most effectively by organizations that have the vision, the courage and the determination to re-organize around Scrum and emerge new structures around Scrum, potentially even a completely new organization. It will certainly require much courage of practitioners, regardless of their role, function or position, to step up and help their organizations and leadership overcome the fear to touch, update and re-think the organizational structures, procedures and constructs around Scrum.

It might require a select, new generation of visionaries and pioneers (of the kind that got us out of the waterfall trap). If enough practitioners move their particular instances of Scrum downfield we will, in turn, collectively and bottom-up, start moving the global movement of Scrum downfield.

The journey is far from over.

> Scrum emerged as the gorilla of the Agile family of methods. Scrum is the de facto standard against which to measure and to oppose. Or to join.

2.4 FRAMEWORK, NOT METHODOLOGY

Scrum, having its roots in new product development theory [Takeuchi & Nonaka, 1986], is designed to help teams create, deliver and sustain complex products in turbulent circumstances via self-organization. Scrum adds the scientific method of empiricism to better deal with complexity and unpredictability to this principle of self-organization. 'Empiricism' and 'self-organization' are the essential management principles embedded in Scrum. They form Scrum's DNA, the core beliefs for a Scrum ecosystem to be shaped upon.

Scrum replaces the industrial, plan-driven approach with well-considered, opportunistic experimentation thriving on the cognitive, creative abilities of its players. The definition of the Scrum framework only holds a bare minimal set of mandatory elements, making each element essential. Breaking Scrum's base design by leaving out one or more elements is likely to cover up problems, instead of revealing and tackling them.

The purpose of empiricism via Scrum is to help people perform inspections and adaptations upon transparency of the work being undertaken and results being produced. Scrum foresees frequent reality checks to assure the best possible decisions about the future. Scrum reminds all involved of the necessity to regularly adjust, adapt, change and show flexibility. All rules, principles and values of the framework serve this purpose.

Scrum, through its minimalistic design, has no exhaustive and formal prescriptions on how to design and plan the behavior of all players, nor does Scrum lay out their expected behavior against time, let alone how the work must be documented, maintained and stored. Scrum has no upfront rules for instructions of document types and deliverables to be produced. Neither does Scrum instruct the exact time of their production. Instead of installing, thriving and relying on handovers, toll gates and control meetings, Scrum exposes them as a major source of delays, waste and disrespect. Yet, it is left up to the organization to de-install them (or not) as Scrum is adopted.

Scrum has its roots in the world of software development. In that world, 'methodologies' are by design composed of stringent and mandatory sequences of steps, processes and procedures, implementing predefined algorithms and executors for each step, process or procedure. This holds the promise of success when the prescriptions are followed. As such, 'methodologies' replace the creativity, autonomy and intellectual powers of people with components like phases, tasks, must-do practices and patterns, executable techniques and digital tools. Obedience to a methodology in a cognitive environment however only serves to ensure formal coverage for blame, not success in terms of working results and value delivered. Such methodologies depend on high degrees of predictability to have a high yield. Complex product development does not have those high degrees of predictability. It is even more unpredictable than it is predictable.

Scrum is the opposite of such a big collection of interwoven mandatory components and maximal set of complete prescriptions. Scrum is not a methodology. Scrum replaces a pre-programmed, algorithmic approach with a heuristic one, with respect for people and self-organization to deal with unpredictability and effectively address complex challenges.

If Scrum is referred to as a 'process', it certainly cannot be as a process of the repeatable kind. That is a challenge to explain because the term 'process' typically invokes a sense of algorithmic and predictable steps, repeatable actions and enforceable top-down control; the sort of expectations that are typical for a…methodology.

If referred to as a 'process', then Scrum is to be understood as a *servant* process, not a *commanding* process. What works best for all involved players and their work processes emerges from the use of Scrum, not from a dictate by Scrum's definition. Players discover the work required to close the gap between an observable result and an envisioned outcome, with the observed result exhibiting the characteristics of the end-product. Scrum is a process that helps surface the most effective process, practices and structures. Scrum creates the boundaries to help discover a way of working that is continuously adaptable to everybody's actual context and current circumstances. Scrum is a . . . framework.

> The framework of Scrum sets the bounded environments for people to act and decide what the best possible action is within those boundaries.

■ 2.5 PLAYING THE GAME

Scrum, as a *framework* for Agile development, was designed to optimize the creation of *valuable* products and services in turbulent enterprise, organizational, business and market circumstances, to derive value from such complex challenges.

Scrum requires much discipline from its players, while leaving plenty of room for personal creativity and context-specific tactics. The rules of the game are based upon respect for the people-players through a subtle and balanced distribution of accountability. Respecting the rules of the game, not taking shortcuts on its rules and roles or short-circuiting the empirical grounds of the game, delivers the most joy and greatest benefits for the players as well as the best results for the users and for the enterprise.

The game board of Scrum shows all that is required to play the game: the players, the artifacts, the events, the main principles and the values of the game of Scrum. The rules of Scrum bind these elements together.

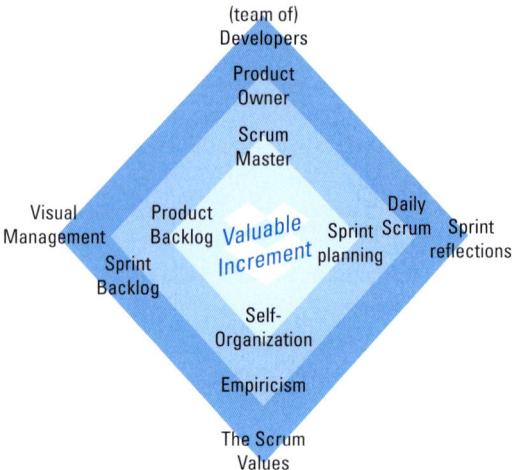

Figure 2.5 The Scrum Game Board

2.5.1 Players and Accountabilities

Scrum organizes its players around three peer accountabilities:

- Product Owner;
- (team of) Developers;
- Scrum Master.

The combination of these accountabilities is known as the *Scrum Team*.

As each accountability complements the other ones, collaboration is the key to success.

Product Owner is a one-person player role upholding the business perspective in the creative development process. A Product Owner forms a bridge between all stakeholders and users and the *(team of) Developers*, a multi-person player role. Although a Product Owner may have strategic product management tasks beyond the Scrum Team, it is important that the

Product Owner actively engages with the other team players regularly and repeatedly.

The Product Owner assures that a *Product Backlog* exists. The Product Owner manages the Product Backlog based on the product vision as a long-term compass. A product vision captures *why* the product exists. From a product vision, specific Product Goals can be derived, which are added to the Product Backlog. A product is a tangible or non-tangible good, service, device or experience serving specific users. When adopting Scrum, it is crucial to know what the 'product' is; its boundaries, its consumers and stakeholders and how it provides value.

The Product Backlog shows all of the work envisioned for the product being created and sustained. This may comprise functional ambitions, non-functional expectations, enhancements, fixes, patches, ideas, updates and other types of work. If anybody wants to know what work is identified and planned for the product, they only have to look at the Product Backlog. Product Backlog is the primary source of work and progress in Scrum.

The Product Owner orders the items in the Product Backlog to optimize the flow of value and expresses their business expectations and ideas. The Product Owner manages the game budget to optimize the balance of value, effort and time.

The Scrum players perform all end-to-end activities required to turn items from the Product Backlog, expressed and ordered by the Product Owner, into releasable versions of product. 'Development' applies to all these activities; all work to be undertaken to create an *Increment* of product within a Sprint. Depending on the context and the product, this might include the creation of test cases, testing, programming, documentation, integration, release activities, etc. It is all of the work necessary to guarantee that an Increment is in a usable state no later than by the end of a Sprint, that it can technically be released to the users and consumers of the product or service. This state of the Increment is called 'Done'. The qualities and criteria that make out this state, and thus drive the development work to be undertaken and the skills required in the team of Developers, are captured in a *definition of Done*. Only Done Increments can be released. Throughout a Sprint, multiple Increments could be created. The definition of Done is not a function of the skills available in a team of Developers, or the tools and practices applied. It is the other way round: skills, tools and practices are a function of the definition of Done.

The development standards of the team describe how the implementation is performed. These standards guarantee the level of quality needed to release regularly. And they provide the right transparency to the way the game is being played.

The players doing the development work set the cost or effort indication on Product Backlog items. They are also the ones to select the amount of work that is assumed doable in a Sprint at the start of that particular Sprint. The evolving effort indications on Product Backlog can be compared with proven experience to make a *forecast* of Product Backlog for a Sprint.

Scrum Master is a one-person player role acting as a game master to guide the team and all involved in the organization. A Scrum Master advises, teaches, coaches and mentors all in understanding, respecting, knowing and applying the rules of the game of Scrum. If Scrum Master is a 'coach', then it should be in the sense of the coach of a sports team (not a personal or a life coach). The Scrum Master makes sure that the rules of the game are well understood by all involved and that any elements that hinder or block the team in its progress and cannot be tackled through self-organization are removed. Such elements are called *Impediments* in Scrum.

The Scrum Master induces the continual desire to become better players. The Scrum Master is successful by helping others make better use of Scrum. The core accountability is to guide self-organization toward the iterative-incremental creation of valuable outcomes.

2.5.2 Time

The time-boxed iterations in the game of Scrum are called *Sprints* to reflect that it concerns an effort over a short period of time with a strong focus. A Sprint is about players focusing on achieving the next game level, the *Sprint Goal*, with minimal external disruptions, not about exhausting the people involved.

All work in Scrum is organized in Sprints. Scrum has no typecasted Sprints, Sprints designated to specific types of development, as the goal of *each* Sprint is to deliver a valuable piece of work, a (product) *Increment*. A Sprint's duration is never more than four weeks and typically takes one to four weeks.

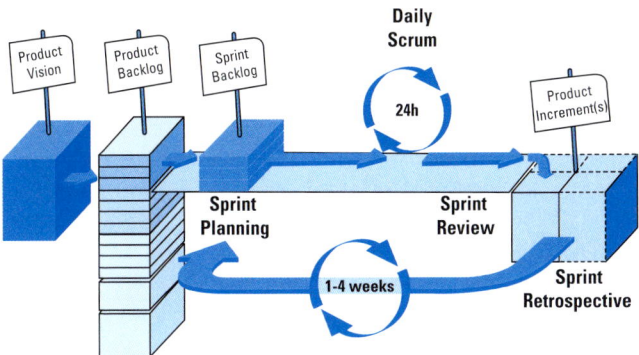

Figure 2.6 Overview of a Scrum Sprint

As a container event, the Sprint encapsulates the other Scrum events. Every event is time-boxed and is an opportunity to respond quickly and collectively to new opportunities and adapt to any changes and evolutions:

- Sprint Planning;
- Daily Scrum;
- Sprint Review;
- Sprint Retrospective.

Every Sprint begins with a *Sprint Planning* event where work from the current Product Backlog ('what') is pulled into the Sprint. The team selects the amount of work it deems feasible for the Sprint, thereby anticipating the work needed to create releasable output as stated in the definition of Done. The selected work is a *forecast* that represents the insights of the team at the time of selection. The accuracy of the forecast might be slightly increased by comparing the amount of work that was on average completed in past Sprints with the team's capacity for the current Sprint. Details and ambitions are discussed with the Product Owner.

The selected work is designed, analyzed and elaborated into an actionable work plan for the time-boxed Sprint, the *Sprint Backlog* ('how'). Meanwhile the Scrum Team defines, refines or resets the overarching objective for the Sprint, the *Sprint Goal* ('why'). The Sprint Goal is a result of Sprint Planning and expresses what makes the Sprint worth the energy and the investment. It can be an envisioned state of the product or some other meaningful outcome of the Sprint. Sprint Planning never takes more than eight hours.

After the expiration of the time-box of Sprint Planning, or when achieving the goal of the event, work starts upon the collaboratively created plan. To manage and follow up on this development work, a short, daily event called the *Daily Scrum* is held. It is a right-time planning event. The plan of the upcoming work for achieving the Sprint Goal is optimized based upon the actual progress within the Sprint. The adaptation is captured in an update of the Sprint Backlog, which is a living artifact. The progress based upon the amount of actually remaining work is visualized. If the actual progress impacts the forecast, for better or for worse, the Product Owner is consulted. The Daily Scrum never takes more than 15 minutes.

As the Sprint progresses, an Increment of the product or service emerges from the collaborative work. If work is 'Done', meaning that it complies with the definition of Done, and is deemed useful, then it can be considered as an Increment that can be released. Nobody external to the team instructs the team on how to proceed or who should be doing what specific work within the Sprint. The team is self-managing.

At the end of the Sprint, the work resulting from the Sprint and the way of working during the Sprint are reflected upon.

The Increment is inspected in a *Sprint Review* session to check on the functional fitness to release it, or the actual usage if it was already released. The Product Owner assures a high level of transparency by presenting Product Backlog evolutions against the Product Goal, as derived from the long-term product vision. While reviewing a product Increment, the attendees, i.e. minimally the Scrum Team and its (key) stakeholders, share desired changes, feedback and evolutionary insights. The goal is to learn about the next work to tackle. This information is processed into the Product Backlog, while understanding that the timing to address them depends on the Product Owner's ordering and the team's sustainable progress. Sprint Review never takes more than four hours.

The Sprint is concluded with a *Sprint Retrospective* in which the Scrum Team inspects and reflects upon the complete 'process'. The event covers all aspects of the work, like suitability to release the product, value delivered, technology, social aspects, the Scrum process, development practices, collaboration, product quality, team engagement, etc. The event is basically about establishing what went well, where there is room for improvement and what experiments might be conducted in order to learn and build a better product. The Scrum Team might decide on preservations, adjustments, experiments and improvements for this purpose in the next Sprint. Sprint Retrospective never takes more than three hours.

Sprint length is best kept steady over several Sprints for reasons of cadence and minimal stability. It is the heartbeat of development and it's useful for the team to understand how much work can be done during a Sprint.

The past performance of a team, in the sense of the amount of work that got done in a Sprint, is sometimes called *Velocity*. Velocity is an indication of the amount of Done work a team was able to create in past Sprints. Velocity is the sum of units of effort or cost that got Done in a Sprint and is typical to one team and one team's composition.

The Sprint length is rightsized for capitalizing on emerging and previously unforeseen business opportunities. The collaborative Sprint Review provides the Product Owner with the best possible information on how additional Sprints can further improve the value that the product delivers and make the best possible progress towards the next Product Goal.

The Sprint length may also depend on how long a team can work without consulting with stakeholders at the Sprint Review. The Sprint Review is an opportunity to adapt to new strategic directions or market evolutions. A team will suffer from reduced learning and adaptation opportunities when not consulting with stakeholders regularly. Sprints may be shorter than four weeks, but never longer.

> Scrum only knows Sprints and the goal of each Sprint is to deliver at least one working version of product, an Increment. Inspections of working versions of product are considered the only measure of progress.

2.5.3 Managing Progress

Overall progress of work is tracked and managed visually for adaptation and forecasting purposes. Looking into the uncertain future is based upon the proven, observed past.

In order to uphold the opportunity to adapt to reality and make forward-looking decisions, always taking unpredictability into account, the remaining work is re-assessed regularly and honestly:

- *Sprint*: The progress within a Sprint is minimally tracked on a daily basis, around the time of the Daily Scrum. The Sprint Backlog always holds the most accurate, realistic plan for the work remaining to achieve the Sprint Goal.
- *Product*: The progress at the level of the Product (Backlog), e.g. towards a Product Goal, is discussed at the Sprint Review. The units that apply when assessing progress are team, Sprint and value (over individuals, tasks, estimates and velocity). The proven progress of past Sprints gives a forecasted delivery date for releases, individual features or feature sets.

The classic Scrum approach to visualize progress is a *Burn-down Chart*, a graph showing the evolution of remaining work:

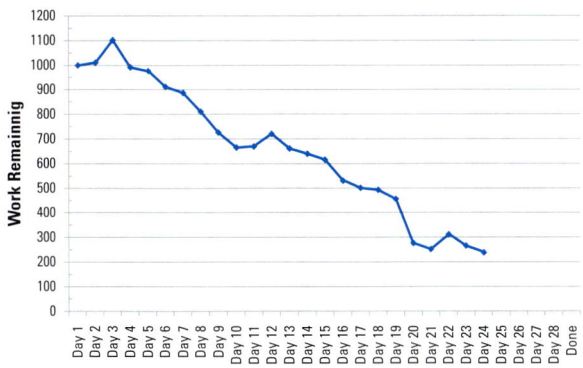

Figure 2.7 Example of a Sprint Burn-down Chart

However, the players decide on the best way to visually manage and represent progress. This may be a burn-down chart, a physical Scrum board, a Burn-up Chart (e.g. in value), or it could be a cumulative flow diagram to better visualize the flow of work:

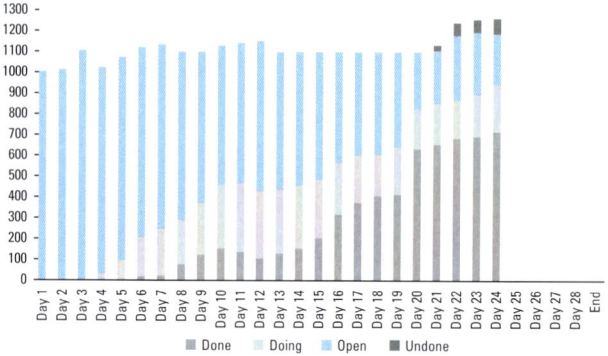

Figure 2.8 Example of a Cumulative Flow Diagram

2.5.4 The Value of the Product Backlog

The value of the Product Backlog lies not in completeness, precision, detail or perfection, nor in capturing every possible requirement in every possible detail against every possible timing horizon. The value of the Product Backlog lies in transparency, in providing direction and uncovering opportunities to create value, in making clear what the Product Owner envisions addressing in order to create a minimally viable and valuable product (Increment) and achieve a specific Product Goal. The Product Backlog brings out into the open all work, development, dependencies and constraints that have to be dealt with.

Product Backlog is an ordered list of ideas, features and options to bring a product to life and subsequently sustain, evolve and grow it. The list is bound to include capabilities, functionalities and features, but can also hold experiments, hypotheses, fixes, maintenance work, architectural work,

work to be spent on security, scalability, stability, performance, etc. The type of work is partially connected to the phase in the product life cycle. At the time of the creation of an item on the Product Backlog, the item is assumed to be valuable or to be contributing to the ability to uphold or add value.

Every item on the Product Backlog holds just enough detail to make clear the value that it represents. A Product Backlog item is intentionally incomplete to encourage additional and explicit discussions. It is a placeholder for deeper discussion at the right time.

The Product Owner has accountability over the Product Backlog and the included Product Goal. A Product Owner, however, takes into account technical and development aspects and input. And a Product Owner also takes into account dependencies, non-functional requirements and organizational expectations.

The Product Backlog is gradually refined, thereby introducing incremental management of product possibilities:

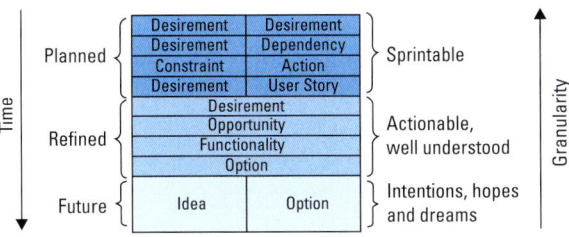

Figure 2.9 Incremental Evolution of Product Backlog

Product Backlog is a living artifact. As development progresses, it is adjusted and updated. The Product Owner continuously orders and re-orders it. Product Backlog being 'ordered' means that there is a clear sequence of items, and not just groups of items with the same priority.

Continuously adhering to 'just enough' descriptions and designs of the work and leaving out unnecessary details ensures that no excessive money and time are wasted if the item ultimately isn't created, is implemented much later or is implemented in a different fashion. Product Backlog shows the next Product Goal which can be used to group items, features and non-functional requirements into cohesive feature sets.

Regardless of the type of items on your Product Backlog, beware of the "First-time right delusion", the belief that perfect product versions can be created in one run, without tweaks, updates and changes to what was previously built, without changes based upon the feedback of the people that actually use the product. A dangerous belief connected to the use of the term 'requirement' is that what is needed is already known prior to its creation and release, without the (in)validation of this assumption by actual usage. After all, there is a reason why the term 'backlog' was chosen. It holds an implicit suggestion that what is to be created might already be outdated when it is released.

I like the term 'desirement' to describe the granularity of a Product Backlog item. The level of description and detail of a Product Backlog item lies somewhere between what is a desire and what used to be a requirement. A 'desire' is too fuzzy to work on. A (traditional) 'requirement' is typically over-specified and over-detailed, which impedes the optimal use of technology, blocks the ability to capitalize on synergies between different functions and is a waste of money in situations of even minimal turbulence or change.

Items move in their ordering from Product Backlog via Sprint Backlog into usable Increments. While the ordering of the Product Backlog depends upon a complex combination of factors like cost/effort, dependencies, priority, cohesion and consistency, it is essential to consider the assumed value of a Product Backlog item.

Core factors for a Product Backlog item are cost *and* value:

- *Cost*: The cost, or effort, of a Product Backlog item is generally expressed in an abstract and relative unit. Past Sprints show how much work, expressed in the chosen unit, was on average converted into working Increments. Upon this empirical given, an expectation can be created of when an item on the future Product Backlog might become available. It is a forecast and doesn't move the players into the realm of exact predictions, because any such future projection is constrained by today's knowledge and circumstances and unknown future changes of the Product Backlog. While the Product Owner is accountable for its ordering, the team of Developers is responsible for its sizing.
- *Value*: An important Agile principle is "to satisfy the customer through early and continuous delivery of valuable software" [Beck, et.al., 2001]. This is why Product Backlog should primarily be ordered for value (while exposing factors that enhance or obstruct the flow of value—like goals, dependencies and constraints). An attribute for (business) value on a Product Backlog item serves as an indicator of how much value it presumably brings. This is balanced against the cost or effort required. A value attribute can be a relative or a calculated indication. It can be money or a more abstract expression of importance. The value of a Product Backlog item can also be indirect, in the sense that not picking it up might undercut the value of the system or even the organization, may lead to negative value or undermine the future ability to create value.

Focusing on value helps Product Owners and their stakeholders move away from the (false) idea that a product must be complete before even considering whether to release it. Everybody's focus shifts from complete products to minimal marketable product releases that offer value and the minimal work it takes to effectively deliver to the marketplace.

> Product Backlog is all the plan that Scrum requires. If needed, it even holds all the information to make forecasts about scope and time. A Product Backlog item needs the right attributes to be ordered, more than just being prioritized.

2.5.5 The Importance of Done

The empiricism of Scrum only functions well with transparency. Transparency is about information being available for the inspector-players, but also requires common standards to work against and to inspect upon. The definition of Done serves the transparency required in Scrum over the work to be done and the work actually done.

In the definition of Done the qualities and criteria are expressed that an Increment of product must meet in order to be considered fit to be released to and used by its end-users. The definition of Done holds the product qualities and – often - the activities, criteria, tasks and work that need to be performed for a piece of product to be of such production quality. 'Done' is what the team is committed to regarding the Increment. The definition of Done is also essential at Sprint Planning to understand and plan the work needed to create a usable, releasable Increment.

The definition of Done should be known by all players. All work to achieve the level of Done is performed within a Sprint. All skills and expertise needed to achieve this are required within the team. A release decision or the inspection of an Increment at the Sprint Review should not be constrained by unknown or undone development work.

Transparency means not only visible, but also understandable. The content of the definition of Done should be self-explanatory.

An organization that thrives and depends on products and services can be expected to have a definition of product qualities in place and to express such to all involved players through standards, guidelines, rules, service levels and other expectations. A professional organization defines quality. Teams of professional product developers are an integral part of an organization, rather than being isolated gangs of thug coders. They can be expected to adhere to the overarching product standards as set by the organization.

If, as can be expected, a minimal definition of Done is provided by the organization (covering development, engineering, quality or operations areas as needed), it can still be expanded with context-specific elements, like the type of product and its life cycle phase, a release, technology. In the absence of organizational guidelines, professionals can be expected to create an appropriate definition of Done for their work anyhow.

Through an agreed definition of Done, quality is at the heart of Scrum. No undone work is part of an Increment. No undone work is put into production. *Ever.* From the inspection of the Increment based upon the definition of Done, the collaborative conversation at the Sprint Review might include quality and requirements with regards to the definition of quality in the organization. This helps the team consider the appropriateness of the definition of Done at the subsequent Sprint Retrospective and include all that is actually possible, and more, while considering the feedback from the stakeholders.

A definition of Done can't be cut short by forces outside of the team. Although dependencies on other teams, external systems or interfaces might lead to re-ordering the work on the Product Backlog, professionals prefer to make progress and implement strategies to increase the independence of their team even when this does not eliminate the dependence. In a software development environment, a team can use stubs, mock-ups or simulators for non-available systems or non-resolved technical dependencies to achieve this. At the same time, all remain aware that the work is not really Done, because it is not releasable. There is an unpredictable amount of work hidden in the system (to make the product work against the actual external system or interface) that must be performed at some point in order to have an actually usable product. In the meantime, the decision to release is blocked. Fortunately, the Sprint Review ultimately reveals this information of dependencies to stakeholders too, so the chances are greater that appropriate actions will be taken within or beyond the organization.

> The definition of Done reveals all the work required and performed within a Sprint to be able to release early and often to the marketplace.

2.6 CORE PRINCIPLES

The Scrum Game Board in figure 2.5 not only shows the mandatory elements of Scrum bound together by the rules of Scrum but also the two main management principles underlying Scrum:

- Self-organization covers the 'people' aspect of Scrum; *and*
- Empiricism (aka 'empirical process control') covers the 'process' aspect of Scrum.

These two management principles are inseparable and form Scrum's DNA.

Although Scrum has been massively adopted around the world, the focus has been and is still very much on the 'process' part of its DNA, the empirical process. Its 'people' part, self-organization, remains undervalued. Yet, they go hand in hand. Both are needed to optimally tackle complex problems and challenges. We need to get the balance right to get the most from our instances of Scrum. A Scrum Master can be expected to act as someone who not only cares about Scrum, but also about the people within the process. A Scrum Master can be expected to act as a Scrum Caretaker, in line with my self-chosen 'title'.

2.6.1 Self-organization

Scrum thrives on the daily collaboration across the three peer accountabilities, with all players demonstrating the collaboractive stance.

The Scrum Team is a self-organizing unit of people, which holds that they form an organized group around a (shared) challenge or problem without external work plans or instructions being imposed on them.

Self-organization is not about delegation. Self-organization *is*. It happens. As any human individual has the inherent quality to self-organize, self-organization doesn't need enabling or empowerment, or a higher authority to grant it. The room to actually self-organize requires the removal of the many existing organizational barriers that prevent people from communicating, interacting, achieving insights and collaborating directly. This is how external authorities are most effective: by removing organizational or procedural barriers that impede people applying their natural ability to self-organize in their professional environment.

Self-organization is not about anarchy or limitless freedom. Self-organization happens within and requires boundaries. The Scrum rules form one of the primary boundaries within which a team self-organizes. As a minimum expression of self-organization, Scrum Teams are *self-managing* in the sense that they devise, plan, execute and track all their work in Sprints without external forces intervening:

- The Product Owner interacts with users, stakeholders and product management to identify the most valuable work and relies on the cross-functional development skills and disciplines of the team for the actual delivery of it in Increments of product.
- The team of Developers collaboratively selects work as ordered and expressed by the Product Owner for a Sprint, devises and manages the actionable activities to implement this forecast and re-plans the work on a daily basis within the time-boxed Sprint to optimize the outcome against the Sprint Goal.
- The Scrum Master has no direct interest in scope, budget, delivery or tasks but coaches and facilitates the other players and the ecosystem within which they operate in using Scrum to manage these factors.

People organized in teams have the highest cohesion, deepest trust and most effective interconnections when the team size numbers around five to seven. Although Scrum expresses an expectation of team size to be ten or fewer people, there's no formal process need to enforce this. Beyond being merely self-managing, teams can be *self-designing* as an expression of self-organization. A team can adjust team size and the number of teams for optimal performance autonomously. There is no external body that knows how to organize better than the people actually undertaking the work.

In his book '*Drive*' [Pink, 2009] Daniel Pink elaborates on the social research that shows what truly motivates people. Once the matter of money and other extrinsic motivators is off the table, 'self-directiveness' (or 'autonomy'), the ability for people to direct their own work, is one of three crucial motivators in cognitive, creative work. 'Mastery' and 'purpose' are the other two. Together they make out what Pink identifies as the third drive, the model for human motivation that comes after the first drive of survival and the second drive of industrial-like Taylorist schemes implementing 'carrots and sticks' rewards. The self-organization of Scrum, rooted in new product development theory [Takeuchi & Nonaka, 1986], is thus confirmed as crucial for the motivation of people in creative work requiring cognitive skills. From the perspective of neuroscience, we know that as a part of good social bonding people need a sense of certainty and fairness too. The SCARF model lists the properties needed in any environment for human beings to prosper: Status (connected to 'mastery'), Certainty, Autonomy, Relatedness (connected to 'purpose') and Fairness [Rock, 2008].

However, autonomy and self-organization are not magical solutions to all problems. Some problems go beyond the self-organizing capabilities of a team. Scrum calls these 'impediments'.

The general definition of an impediment is an "*obstruction; hindrance; obstacle*". An impediment in Scrum is a factor that blocks the team in its creation of valuable versions of product in a Sprint or restricts the team in achieving its intrinsic level of progress. It is the accountability of the Scrum Master to assure that impediments are removed, whether it is done by the Scrum Master alone or by the Scrum Master helping others do it.

The Scrum concept of 'impediments', however, is not a replacement for the traditional escalation procedures. An impediment is only an impediment if it surpasses the self-organizing capabilities of the team; if it cannot be tackled within the self-organizing ecosystem that a team is.

Let's illustrate this with the example of a team conflict, a conflict between team members.

Working as a team inevitably includes getting to know each other, building rapport while building product together, exploring different ways to collaborate, finding consensus over differing ideas, outgrowing the desire for personal heroism, transcending individual skills and expertise. In her book '*Coaching Agile Teams*', Lyssa Adkins elaborates on 'constructive disagreement' as a necessity for teams [Adkins, 2010]. This minimal level of conflict connects to the 'built-in instability' observed and described by Takeuchi and Nonaka as the fertile ground for successful new product development [Takeuchi & Nonaka, 1986]. It is a natural part of the freedom given to a group of people to jointly discover the best ways to move forward, in the absence of an external authority that prescribes the solution. Conflicts are a natural part of people working as a team. Productive dissent is an essential part of self-organization.

In many organizations the biggest problem with 'conflict' however is the absence of conflict, a situation of team members not feeling the safety and therefore not willing to speak up and share their viewpoints. It leads to a situation of artificial harmony with all team members seemingly agreeing all of the time. It is a sign of the absence of the minimal level of conflict needed for fruitful collaboration, self-organization and capitalizing on the collective intelligence of the team.

On the other hand, a team might have problems in resolving an inner-team conflict and call the conflict an impediment, expecting the Scrum Master to 'remove' it for them. In other words, they expect the Scrum Master to resolve the conflict.

One should wonder what the real problem is in this situation.

Is it the Scrum Master's role to resolve the conflict? Or would that be an undesired intervention in the self-organizing ecosystem, undermining future honesty, learning and self-improvement? How can the Scrum Master augment self-organization? Is it by presenting teams with an external decision that they can use as an excuse to hide behind?

A Scrum Master, as the promoter of Scrum and self-organization, seeks to establish an environment of safety for a team to tackle their problems themselves and offers any tools, training and insights on how best to do this, on how to self-develop. A Scrum Master helps teams enter and remain in a state of productive dissent. If needed, additional, external facilitation can be involved.

A potentially important, real impediment to self-organization for a Scrum Master to address is the lack of a dedicated team space. A dedicated team space is indispensable for collaborative, creative teamwork, where office spaces or cubicles are absolutely unfit for it.

Self-organizing teams, in order to function properly and grow in terms of effectiveness and performance, need a shared workspace for their intense interactions and collaboration. A team needs its own workspace to optimize dialogue, communication and collaboration. There can be no barriers that obstruct the flow of information, not of a physical nature (think: cubicles) and not of a mental nature (think: open office). A shared workspace facilitates a team and its members in making fast decisions.

Although not mandatory, physical co-location is most optimal from a team dynamics perspective. But even when not working co-located, a team needs a virtual shared workspace with modern communication facilities to overcome the physical distance as effectively as possible. All overhead, administrative work and external meetings are kept to a bare minimum. The team keeps a focus on value-adding activities.

Such a shared workspace includes the storage of information because teams require fast access to all relevant information in order to create, maintain and share it, and speed up all decisions that will be made upon it. That's why teams also prefer *visual management* techniques and why a shared workspace has many *information radiators* [Cockburn, 2002]. Information radiators limit the time to convey information within the team as a unit. This applies to all information the team deems appropriate to visualize, such as designs and models, impact analyses, impediments, the definition of Done, the development standards, product and market information. A task overview, team definitions, standards and agreements, process artifacts and progress trends are made accessible and visible within the shared workspace; on white boards, flip charts or other (potentially digital) means. Within the room all information is readily available and made transparent; the room *radiates* it towards the interested reader.

The information is not static. At any point in time the current state of affairs is shown, where that current state might be used to project forecasts for the future. The reader is not forced to enter electronic systems, get authorizations, authenticate, search for information, search for the most recent version of it, or even enquire about it. Teams maintain all crucial information in this visualized way to *share* it within and beyond the team members and use it to inspect and adapt.

> The ability to self-organize is an inherent quality of people although self-organization is most effective when teams have a dedicated workspace.

2.6.2 Empirical Process Control

New product development is a complex activity in itself and it serves to create and evolve complex products in complex circumstances.

One perspective on the degree of 'complexity' is the number of parameters, variables and events that influence an activity and its progression. In product development some of the more commonly known parameters are user expectations and requirements, skills, availability and experience of people organized in teams, technology, integrations, timelines and funding, market conditions and competition, regulations and dependencies. Beyond the known parameters are the unknown ones.

However, it is not only the number of known parameters that is important, but also the *available* knowledge as well as the *required* knowledge of these parameters. *What is the level of detail required to comprehend a variable as well as the future behavior of that variable?* Even if a parameter is known, the level of detail may be too deep to be able to fully understand it. And then, of course, the behavior of the parameter is still not necessarily predictable. A known variable may still behave completely differently than what was expected and known variables might cause unknown effects on each other.

Besides the impact of the broader environment and external circumstances, 'complexity' is already dependent on the nature of the activity itself. The exact and detailed outcomes of product development are hard to describe and predict before or even at the beginning of the actual work. Next to 'what' needs to be accomplished, there's also 'how' to perform the work. The combined steps, tasks and activities that make out creative development work aren't predictable with a high degree of precision because they are not repeatable. Every non-mechanistic or non-industrial product is unique. It also typically involves working with technology. And technology evolves constantly and is dependent on the particularity of an individual organization's environment. And let's not forget that people, self-organized in teams, perform the work. The involvement and engagement of people is dependent on many circumstances and people are not robots or resources.

The degree of dynamism of a problem or activity requires the right process to be in place in order to have the right form of control over the activity:

- In an *open loop system*, a number of steps are performed in a single run in order to lead to a pre-defined, predicted result. It requires all of the variables to be gathered upfront because they need to be presented to the system as input and cannot change as the system processes them. In order to be able to predict output and the elapse time, this type of process control assumes a high degree of predictability of all variables that influence the process as well as of the process activities themselves.

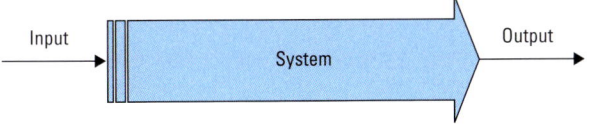

Figure 2.10 Open Loop System

To gain control over larger or complex problems with open loop thinking, subsystems are typically created and linked where each subsystem is a separate open loop system. The input of each subsystem is the output of the previous subsystem. In situations of increased turbulence and frequent change, deviations and variances accumulate across the chain of subsystems, inherently far beyond acceptable levels and only to be detected at the end of the final subsystem.

Predictive plans are expressions of the industrial paradigm and implementations of open loop thinking. Predictive plans can only include known variables and their *expected* behavior. Predictive plans create the illusion that the behavior of the known variables is precisely understood and that other variables are non-existent. Predictive plans invite lengthy upfront consideration of all elements that should be part of the plan. In a complex context it means attempting to foresee the inherently unforeseeable. In order to control non-predicted variables or unexpected behavior, weighty procedures are required to check, maintain and update the predictive plan.

Open loop thinking and predictive management apply to static problems only.

- In a *closed loop system*, the actual outcome of the system is regularly compared to the desired outcome in order to eliminate or gradually diminish any undesired variances. Not all variables and parameters need to be known precisely and in detail upfront, as the process is self-correcting by adjusting to new or changing parameters. This technique of regular inspections requires and creates transparency. The real situation is exposed for inspection so that the most appropriate adaptations can be undertaken to close the gap between the effective and the expected outcomes. The people performing the inspections, the player-inspectors, need clear and agreed standards in order to carry out their inspections. Hence the need for transparency of the process and all its variables for all players involved.

Adaptive problems, problems that change shape as they are being addressed, require closed loop systems and empirical management. Scrum replaces the open loops of traditional processes with the *empiricism* of closed loop feedback. Scrum implements regular opportunities for inspection and adaptation, so the players can learn from inspections, gather feedback, adjust and improve. Scrum brings reality-based control to complex work.

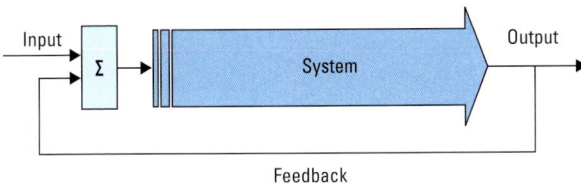

Figure 2.11 Closed Loop System

The simplicity of Scrum is crucial to address complexity. When we say that Scrum is simple, we mean to say that Scrum has a simple set of rules. When we add that Scrum is not easy, we mean to say that it is not easy to stick to Scrum's simplicity, certainly not for organizations with their roots in the industrial paradigm. The idea of Scrum is not to pretend that the problem itself becomes simple by using Scrum and would thus not be complex (anymore). That would be simplistic.

Scrum implements two specific closed-loop feedback cycles. A Sprint forms an 'inspect and adapt' cycle that wraps the 24-hours 'inspect and adapt' of the Daily Scrum:

- At the *Daily Scrum* the progress of development is inspected to plan the upcoming work within the container of the Sprint. This is done against the Sprint Goal as contained in the Sprint Backlog and upon the visually managed progress information. It assures that Developers don't get out of sync with each other and with the Sprint Goal for more than 24 hours.
- A *Sprint* is a cycle that starts with planning activities for the Sprint and ends with reflections on all aspects of the Sprint; *why* the Sprint was undertaken, *what* was actually built (the product Increment) and *how* it was done (the process, the team interactions and the technology).

The events of Scrum set the frequency of the inspection and adaptation, where the artifacts contain the information to be inspected and adapted:

Event	Inspection	Adaptation
Sprint Planning	• Product Backlog (Past performance) (Availabilities) (Retrospective commitments) (Definition of Done)	• Sprint Backlog (Forecast+Plan+Sprint Goal)
Daily Scrum	• Sprint Progress (Towards the Sprint Goal)	• Sprint Backlog (Plan)
Sprint Review	• Product Increment • Product Backlog (& progress toward the Product Goal) • Market & business conditions	• Product Backlog
Sprint Retrospective	• Current Sprint (Value and definition of Done) (Team and collaboration) (Technology and development)	• Next Sprint (Way of working) (Actionable improvements) (Experiments)

Figure 2.12 Empiricism in Scrum

Scrum foresees these formal events as opportunities to inspect the actual situation and adapt to it, so that the art of empiricism is performed no later than at the time of these events. This should not stop players from checking for improvements and progress whenever required. In a world of high dynamism that leads to adopting the Scrum framework it would be very strange if teams did not capitalize as soon as possible on new information and insights that improve their work life.

None of these events was intended for reporting purposes. All events in Scrum are designed to be forward-looking. The ability to adapt defines the level of agility achieved with Scrum.

> Inspection without adaptation is pointless in Scrum. All Scrum events are intended to be forward-looking, as opportunities to shape the future.

■ 2.7 THE SCRUM VALUES

With Scrum, a frame is created within which people and organizations develop a working process that is specific and appropriate to their time and context. Within the boundaries of Scrum, people form organized groups around a common problem or challenge without external work plans or instructions being imposed on them. Next to this principle of *self-organization*, the rules and principles of Scrum all serve *empiricism*, also known as 'empirical process control'. Self-organization and empiricism form Scrum's DNA and combined they form the most suitable approach for addressing complex challenges in complex circumstances.

There is, however, more than these rules and management principles. Ultimately, Scrum is more about behavior than it is about process. Values drive behavior. The framework of Scrum is based upon five core values [Schwaber & Beedle, 2001]. Although these values were not invented as a part of Scrum and are not exclusive to Scrum, they do give direction to the work, behavior and actions in Scrum. The Scrum Values of commitment, focus, openness, respect and courage drive the behavior of the inhabitants of the house of Scrum.

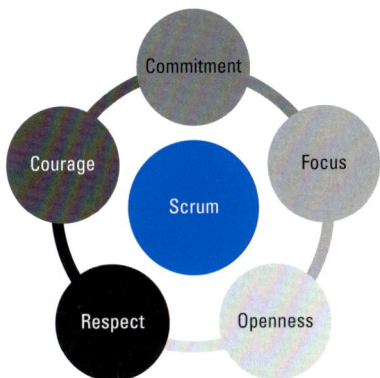

Figure 2.13 The Scrum Values

In a context of Scrum, our decisions, the steps we take, the way we play the game, the practices we include and the activities we undertake within Scrum should all re-enforce these values, not diminish or undermine them, whether it concerns the 'process' or the 'people' aspects of Scrum.

> Scrum is a framework of rules, principles and . . . values.

2.7.1 Commitment

The general definition of 'commitment' is *"the state or quality of being dedicated to a cause, activity, etc."*. It can be illustrated by a team's trainer stating, *"I could not fault my players for their commitment"* (although they might have just lost a game).

This describes exactly how commitment is intended in Scrum. Commitment is about engagement and dedication and applies to the actions and the intensity of the effort. It is not about the final result, as this in itself is often uncertain and unpredictable for complex challenges in complex circumstances.

Yet, there was a widely spread misinterpretation of the word commitment in a context of Scrum. This originates mainly from the past expectation of Scrum that teams should 'commit' to a Sprint. Through the lens of the traditional, industrial paradigm this was wrongly translated into an expectation that all scope selected at Sprint Planning would be completed by the end of the Sprint, no matter what happened. 'Commitment' was wrongly converted into a hard-coded contract.

In the complex, creative and highly unpredictable worlds that Scrum helps us to navigate, a promise to deliver exact, in the sense of precisely predicted, output or scope against time and budget is simply not possible, not even for a Sprint. Too many of the variables that influence the work are unknown or behave in unpredictable ways, even within a Sprint.

To better reflect the original intent and connect more effectively to empiricism, 'commitment' in the context of scope for a Sprint was replaced with 'forecast'.

However, commitment is and remains a core value of Scrum:

The players are committed to the team, to collaborative action and thus to a collaboractive stance. They commit to quality. Commit to learn. Commit to do the best they can, every day, with the commitment to work at a sustainable pace. They are committed to the goals they set. They commit to act as professionals. Commit to self-organize. Commit to excellence. Commit to the Agile value statements and principles. Commit to create working versions of product that comply with the definition of Done. Commit to look for improvements. Commit to the Scrum framework. Commit to deliver value. Commit to finish work. Commit to inspect and adapt. Commit to transparency. Commit to productive dissent and challenging the status quo.

2.7.2 Focus

The balanced but distinct accountabilities of Scrum enable all players to focus on their expertise, interests and talents while the focus on overarching ambitions and shared goals invites them to combine, extend and improve their expertise, skills and talents.

The time-boxing of Scrum encourages the players to focus on what's most important now without being bothered by considerations of what might stand a chance of becoming important at some unknown point in the future. They focus on what they know now. YAGNI ('You Ain't Gonna Need It') helps in retaining that focus. The players focus on what is most imminent as the future is highly uncertain and they prefer learning from the present in order to gain experience for future work. They focus on the work needed to get things done. They focus on the simplest thing that might possibly work.

The Sprint Goal gives focus to a period of four weeks, or less. Within that period, the Daily Scrum helps people collaboratively focus on the immediate daily work needed to make the best possible progress towards the Sprint Goal. A Product Goal provides direction and focus across multiple Sprints and helps in finding and keeping direction.

2.7.3 Openness

The empiricism and self-organization of Scrum require transparency, openness and honesty.

The player-inspectors want to check on the real situation in order to make sensible adaptations. The players are open about their work, progress, learnings and problems. But they are also open for the people aspect of work and what working with people involves, acknowledging people to be… people, and not 'resources', robots, cogs or replaceable pieces of machinery.

The players are open to collaborate across disciplines, skills, functions and job descriptions without external procedures or rules of governance dictating that. They are open to collaborate with stakeholders, users, key users and the wider environment. Open in sharing feedback and learning from one another.

They are open for change as the organization and the world in which they operate change; unpredictably, unexpectedly and constantly.

2.7.4 Respect

The broader Scrum ecosystem thrives on respect for people, their professional experience and their personal background. The players respect and strive for diversity. They respect different opinions. They respect each other's skills, expertise and insights. Differences in opinions are respectfully dealt with in a state of productive dissent.

The players respect the wider environment by not behaving as an isolated entity. They respect the fact that customers change their mind. They show respect for the sponsors of their initiatives by not building or keeping functions that are never used and that increase the total cost of the product. They show respect by not wasting money on things that are not valuable, not appreciated or might never be implemented or used anyhow. They show respect for users by fixing their problems.

All players respect the Scrum framework. All involved respect the accountabilities of Scrum, whether part of the team or not.

2.7.5 Courage

The players show courage by not building stuff that nobody wants. Courage in admitting that requirements will never be perfect and that no plan can capture reality and complexity.

They show the courage to welcome change and different opinions as a source of inspiration and innovation. Courage to not deliver undone versions of product. Courage in sharing all possible information that might help the team and the organization. Courage in entering a state of productive dissent. Courage in admitting that nobody is perfect. Courage to change direction. Courage to share risks and benefits. Courage to let go of the illusory certainties of the past.

The players show courage in promoting Scrum and enacting its underlying management principles of self-organization and empiricism to deal with complexity. The courage to act on deliberate emergence. The courage to take a decision, act and make progress, not grind to a halt. And even more courage to change that decision.

They show courage in supporting and enacting the Scrum Values.

3 Tactics for a Purpose

The definition of Scrum has gradually evolved via small functional updates [Verheyen, 2023]. The basic elements have largely remained the same since 1998, as have the principles and rules that bind them together.

The purpose is to merely describe 'what' is expected from applying the rules, from an understanding of their 'why', as opposed to instructing 'how' to exactly apply them. Value still is the overarching purpose of the game of Scrum.

The previous chapter describes the *rules* to playing the game of Scrum and the principles and values underlying these rules. The rules leave room for different *tactics* to play the game, tactics that are at any time right-size and can be fitted to context and circumstances. Just as in all games and sports, everyone plays by the same set of rules, yet some are more successful than others. Success depends on many factors, and not all are equally controllable by the players themselves, but success is certainly influenced by the tactics chosen to play the game.

It requires checking out a range of *good* practices and turning selected ones into *best* practices by applying and tuning them to a specific context. When referred to as a 'process', Scrum is a *servant* process, not a *commanding* process. Scrum does not say what practices to apply, or not. Scrum helps discover whether they work but leaves it to the players to keep on doing them or changing them. Tactics are a vital part of Scrum and are vital to playing the game.

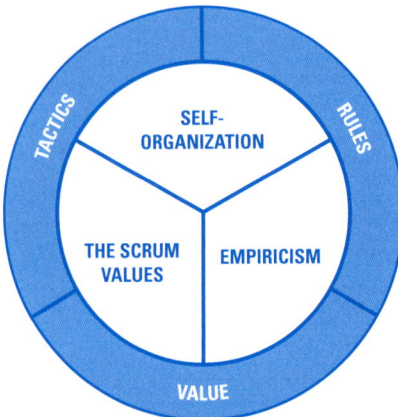

Figure 3.1 The Scrum Vitals

There are many potential tactics to use within Scrum. Good tactics serve the purpose of Scrum. Good tactics re-enforce the Scrum values, rather than undercut them. When such tactics are applied well, the resulting system is still recognizably . . . Scrum. Scrum can wrap many practices.

Let's take a closer look at some examples to clarify and demonstrate what tactics are.

■ 3.1 VISUALIZING PROGRESS

A good illustration of an evolution of the Scrum framework towards more lightness is the elimination of burn-down charts as mandatory.

Looking at the rules of Scrum, including the need for transparency crucial to the empirical process and self-organization, it is clear 'why' it is important to apply visual management techniques. Self-corrective management is difficult to achieve without tracking *and* visualizing progress.

The obligation to use burn-down charts for that purpose (the 'how' of the visualization) was removed from the definition of Scrum. The form or format of the visualization is not prescribed. It is replaced by the mere, but not negligible, expectation that progress on the mandatory Scrum artifacts of Product Backlog and Sprint Backlog is visualized (the 'what' that is expected), for those artifacts to be visually managed.

An example of a Sprint Burn-down chart (figure 2.7) is shown in section 2.5.3 ("Tracking progress"). Sprint Burn-down charts are a great instrument for self-management within a Sprint.

A so-called *Release Burn-down chart* is a way to track and visualize progress for a Product Backlog, part of a Product Backlog or a specific Product Goal. The visualization supports the Product Owner in the interactions with stakeholders, users and the wider product management organization. A Release Burn-down chart and the visual forecast included enable conversations about the balance of time and importance based on actually delivered results.

Burn-down charts are a great tactic to apply and are suitable in many situations. Yet, they are a non-mandatory, good practice.

Yes, it's Scrum if both Product Backlog and Sprint Backlog exist and a visualization of their progress is available, accessible and clear. But there are multiple good practices for such visualization. It may be a burn-down chart with open effort. It may be a Cumulative Flow Diagram, of which figure 2.8 is an example. It may be as simple as a Scrum Board. For the progress

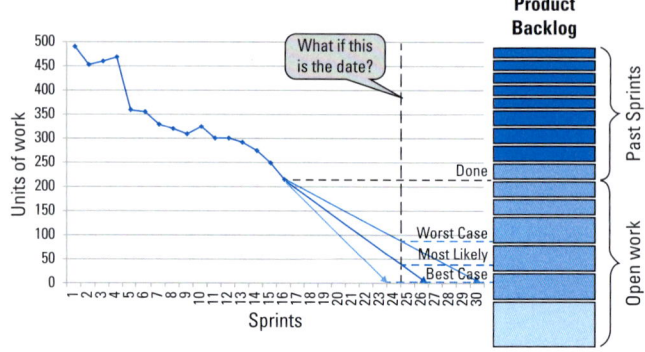

Figure 3.2 Example of a Release Burn-down Chart

at the level of the Product Backlog, it may also be a Burn-up Chart, e.g. in assumed or realized value.

■ 3.2 THE DAILY SCRUM QUESTIONS

Scrum used to suggest that in the Daily Scrum every player answers three questions with regards to the progress of the team towards the Sprint Goal (*Done? Planned? Impediments?*).

But even if the players answer these questions, it can still be just an individual status update. They might just make sure that they simply answer the three questions. It doesn't help much whether they formally answer the three questions, or not, if they don't actually listen and talk to each other. It doesn't help much if they don't surface the information needed to optimize their shared work plan for the next day of work against the Sprint Goal.

Maybe they use the event only as a formal obligation, a mental remainder of the industrial paradigm. Maybe they feel pressured to make sure all their micro-tasks are logged to cover themselves against possible blame. It may be because of people's inability to look beyond the (past) suggestion of Scrum to answer the questions and the expectation to formally comply with the process. Maybe the perceived rules are formally followed without understanding the 'why'. Whatever the reason, however, they miss the opportunity to gain insight into the real situation, to inspect it and to adapt to it, fluently and rapidly.

Inspection without adaptation is pointless in complex and changing environments. The goal of the Daily Scrum is to share information and to re-plan the collective work to ensure the best possible progress. The team sets its own format to do so, within the boundary of keeping it to 15 minutes, or less. That should be the background from which the Daily Scrum is used, regardless of whether these are the questions that are addressed; not blindly go through the questions from a 'best practice' viewpoint.

Did you know that a Daily Scrum is not necessarily a Daily Stand-up?

Daily Stand-up Meetings is the practice described in eXtreme Programming [Beck & Fowler, 2001]. Although they serve the same purpose as the Daily Scrum in Scrum, eXtreme Programming tells participants to do it standing up.

In Scrum there is no obligation to do the Daily Scrum standing up. However, it is a good tactic, especially to focus and keep the time-box within 15 minutes.

■ 3.3 PRODUCT BACKLOG REFINEMENT

Refinement of the Product Backlog is an on-going activity during a Sprint in which the Product Backlog currently ordered for the next Sprints is considered. After all, there is a growing certainty that these items are actually going to be implemented. Although they might still be re-ordered or eliminated, it might be helpful to have a closer look at that work.

As items on a Product Backlog come closer in time, teams might want to unveil dependencies, understand better what is expected from the work, decide on a shared approach for its development or help a Product Owner understand the development impact at a usage or functional level. Collaborative refinement of Product Backlog, and the additional knowledge that emerges from the conversation, increases the chances that the work might actually, or more easily, be pulled into a Sprint when it is presented at a future Sprint Planning.

Product Backlog refinement is not an official event. It has no defined time-box, nor is it defined when or how often it should happen. The ambition of Scrum is to remain simple, yet sufficient. The ambition of Scrum is to help people and teams discover specific practices, tactics, that may or may not be appropriate in their specific context. Product Backlog refinement is an activity that many teams undertake to smoothen their Sprints and reduce turbulence during Sprint Planning and in the first days of a Sprint. A typical feature of Product Backlog refinement activities is that estimates of effort or cost get set or are revised. Other teams may need less precision at Sprint Planning or have a relationship with the Product Owner that's less about upfront accuracy. They cope without it, or do it less formally, do it without explicitly naming or consciously planning this activity.

Product Backlog refinement might be a good tactic to collaboratively manage upcoming Product Backlog. Some can do without however and figure more details out at Sprint Planning.

3.4 USER STORIES

In eXtreme Programming [Beck & Fowler, 2001] requirements are captured in 'User Stories'. User Stories were originally written on index cards and described units of functionality from a user's perspective. Bill Wake, an early practitioner of eXtreme Programming, suggested the 'INVEST' acronym as a simple way to remember and assess whether or not a User Story is well formed: Independent, Negotiable, Valuable, Estimable, Sized appropriately, Testable. The advantage of taking the user's perspective to describe a specific system or application behavior is the focus on the value for that user.

Index cards are easy to move around on, or remove from, a planning board, as an information radiator. Another advantage of using physical index cards for stories is the limited space for textual descriptions and details. It ensures incompleteness by design so that conversation will have to take place. The incompleteness necessitates conversation. More information may be added to the card, like acceptance criteria describing when the Story would be correctly implemented. Such acceptance criteria are typically written on the back of the card. These three Cs of User Stories ("Cards", "Conversation" and "Confirmation") are components that were introduced by Ron Jeffries, another early practitioner of eXtreme Programming.

There is no obligation in Scrum to use the User Story-format for Product Backlog items.

A Product Backlog in Scrum serves to provide transparency to *all* work deemed valuable by the Product Owner. This comprises more than just functional system behaviors. Although the User Story format may be used for other types of requirements than functional, there is no natural fit. Trying to express such requirements as User Stories tends to shift the focus to the syntax instead of the information to be conveyed. User Stories need not even be expressed in the syntax of 'As a (user) I want (story)'.

So, there is the risk of neglecting other important work that needs to be undertaken or the problem of forcing teams to spend more time and energy on using the 'right' format, thus creating waste. However, for functional items on the Product Bocklog, using User Stories can be a good tactic.

■ 3.5 PLANNING POKER

Planning Poker is an estimation technique invented by James Grenning during an eXtreme Programming project where he felt too much time was spent on the exactness of estimates.

In Planning Poker, a team discusses a chunk of work or functionality, after which every team member individually estimates it by picking a value from a set of poker cards. Poker cards typically use an exponential scale like the Fibonacci sequence (1, 2, 3, 5, 8, 13, 21, 34, 55, …) to counter the desire for precision and exactness, and thus restore the idea of an…estimate. All team members keep their choice to themselves until everybody has chosen a value. They then simultaneously reveal their estimates and engage in a conversation. This cycle is repeated until agreement is reached, a sign of the joint understanding of the anticipated effort. Estimates are relative to each other and are expressed in an abstract unit like (Story) points, t-shirt sizing or gummy bears like in early eXtreme Programming projects.

If teams choose to estimate in Scrum, it is required to have honest and unbiased estimates from a collective, cross-functional development perspective. Although not mandatory, Planning Poker is a good tactic for that principle. But the ultimate intention remains to invoke an honest discussion about the estimates, because this results in a good understanding of the work attached to implementing the discussed item.

■ 3.6 EXTREME DEVELOPMENT

The rules of Scrum don't include specific development practices, exact instructions on 'how' to perform the work. As part of transparency and its emphasis on teamwork, Scrum does however absolutely require that development standards are established, agreed and adhered to. Scrum cannot be employed to its full extent if they are lacking.

While the definition of Done is particularly important in assuring that all have a shared understanding of the qualities and state of the work, development practices are needed to collectively and incrementally create Done output, meaning that it complies with the definition of Done, and generates valuable outcomes.

Agile Development entails closing feedback loops regularly and repeatedly within the Sprint, preferably even at a frequency higher than that of the Daily Scrum. It helps in assuring alignment and consistency as well as in catching problems and errors early. Consider the propagation of errors that, if not detected early, potentially endanger proper closure of the Sprint.

With specific practices like Pair Programming, Test-Driven Development, Continuous Integration, Refactoring and Collective (Code) Ownership, eXtreme Programming 'nominates coding as the key activity' [Beck, 2000].

Although the practices from eXtreme Programming are good, non-mandatory practices from a Scrum perspective, software development teams should seriously consider adopting them and turning them into a daily habit. The combination of Scrum and eXtreme Programming is one of those rare mixes of methods where the unique flavors are not lost, but mutually augment each other. I would go as far as to say that Scrum and eXtreme Programming were born for each other.

Let me describe the one development practice from XP that is most overlooked: Pair Programming.

Pair Programming is the practice of two people co-developing a Product Backlog item, which is why I prefer calling it 'Pair Development'. It was very powerful for several teams that I worked with.

Within the time that a pair works together, the individuals take up a different role: 'driver' and 'navigator'. The driver, focused on the code, gets immediate feedback from the navigator, who is minding the overview, the design, the overall direction of the development work. The driver and the navigator switch roles frequently and dynamically. It depends on the code or work at hand, whether either of them has already done this before, whether either has a really great idea, etc.

Obviously, Pair Development necessarily results in a lot of communication, which actually reinforces the need for a dedicated team space. But the combined intelligence of, minimally, two people putting their brains together leads to a simpler and higher quality system. Meanwhile the unwanted (future) effort of rework is prevented. *Waste is prevented.* Because the driver and the navigator don't perform the same work, Pair Development is not more costly than individual development. Ultimately, lighter applications are created with lighter architectures that are easier to maintain and thus have a lower TCO ('Total Cost of Ownership').

Pair Development can be extended to even more people and potentially even the whole team working together on the same Product Backlog item. It leads to WIP ('work in process') being limited drastically and potentially even the establishment of a one-piece flow system in which the WIP is limited to 1. It is always better to close a Sprint with all started work Done, even if the amount of Done work is less than anticipated.

It is mandatory in Scrum to define and devise specific development tactics, the practices to collectively create Done output. The rules of Scrum hold no specific instructions because it is a tactical decision. The practices defined in eXtreme Programming can be applied literally in a software development context or show the way in a different context.

■ 3.7 SPRINT LENGTH

Scrum only defines the maximum length of a Sprint: no more than four weeks. This maximum length ensures that nobody is deprived of the right to adapt the future plans for the product at least every four weeks. Additionally, the team does not stay locked away in the container that is a Sprint for too long, at the risk of losing grip on the changing world outside of the container.

Sprint length holds a balance between retaining focus to get a substantial amount of work done along with the opportunistic adaptiveness, and is weighed against other factors like technological uncertainties and learning opportunities.

In an empirical process like Scrum, control objectives are presented to the system and, via closed loop feedback, results are regularly inspected against these objectives to adapt work materials, tasks, practices and processes. Skilled inspectors, upon the accountabilities defined in Scrum, carry out inspections at an appropriate frequency, so the focus and time required to create valuable output are balanced against the risk of allowing too much variance in the created output.

Next to transparency, frequency is an important factor in empiricism. The Scrum events determine the frequency of the inspections and adaptations in Scrum, with the Sprint being a container event, the outer feedback loop that wraps the feedback loop of the Daily Scrum and the feedback loops of the development practices applied within the Sprint.

Over the years, there is a clear tendency to move to shorter Sprints. Although not a formal obligation, one-week Sprints feel like a minimum.

Let's have a look at this by presuming that a team does one-day Sprints.

All Scrum events, all serving specific opportunities to inspect and adapt, take place in the course of one working day. They happen thus at a very high frequency. When actually trying to have all events, the team spends an unreasonable amount of time inspecting and adapting the tiniest of work packages. This gets in the way of getting substantial amounts of work done and of producing value.

The danger is even higher that a team will focus merely on its daily work and progress. They will no longer take time to inspect and adapt the overall process or probe for ways to improve quality or connect to an overarching goal and objectives. They will just try to get more product out the door, at least every day if not more often.

Sprint length also determines the frequency at which feedback is solicited from the stakeholders about a working version of the product or service. The purpose is to share all information needed to help the Product Owner make decisions about the future of the product. In the case of one-day Sprints, stakeholder buy-in will be nearly impossible to achieve, let alone capturing information to adapt to enterprise, market and strategic changes. The danger is losing sight of the bigger picture.

Moving to one-day Sprints will burn or eliminate the inspection-adaptation mechanisms due to the high frequency at which they will be performed. It is similar to not having proper inspection-adaptation mechanisms in place due to not working in Sprints.

If your business is so volatile that you risk losing opportunities by not releasing frequently enough, consider creating and releasing multiple Increments throughout a Sprint. Nothing in Scrum says you can't. The purpose of time-boxed Sprints and the Sprint Review event remain intact regardless. Sprint Review never was intended as a release gate anyhow.

Setting the Sprint length is a tactical decision, bearing in mind stability, heartbeat and sustainable pace. Like other tactics, it is not set in stone. See how it works and adapt accordingly. Like other tactics, it allows you to tweak and tune your instance of Scrum to your context: the people in your team, your technology stack, product, organization, consumer base, market.

The overall advice is to use Scrum to finally stop the old rat race, to humanize and de-mechanize the workplace. Manage work in Sprints such that it is sustainable, indefinitely.

I do wonder why leadership teams would impose the same Sprint length on all teams within their organization, with all teams starting and ending their Sprints on the same dates, regardless of their context. It is one of the many ways to industrialize your Scrum to death, rather than merely standardize on Scrum. Standardizing on Scrum holds that all teams play by the same rules, while applying different, context-specific tactics.

■ 3.8 SCRUM IN THE LARGE

The mandatory elements of Scrum have been described, as well as the rules to play the game of Scrum, the rules that cohesively tie those elements together. Those rules are independent of the scale at which Scrum is organized.

Scrum promotes simplicity. Scrum promotes clear accountability and peer collaboration to deal with unpredictability and formulate answers to complex problems.

Simplicity, bottom-up accountability and collaboration were not at the core of many enterprises when they enlarged their organizational and work structures, but the industrial paradigm was, including its disrespect for the 'workers'. The main challenge in applying Scrum in the large lies not in fitting Scrum into such existing structures, but to revise the existing structures via a bottom-up understanding, implementation and iterative-incremental growth of Scrum, while keeping the base rules of the game intact and respecting them. Adapt the organization to Scrum, not the other way around.

There are some tactics that allow Scrum to be played on a larger scale, depending on the context.

3.8.1 Single-team Scrum

The simplest situation for managing a product or service with Scrum is to capture the work deemed valuable for the product's consumers in one Product Backlog, with one team delivering Increments of product in time-boxed Sprints.

As "Done" is defined by the product and therefore defines the team's skills, the team turns Product Backlog items into one or more releasable product Increments per Sprint. The team self-manages its work via Sprint Backlog and safeguards direction and alignment via the Daily Scrum. The Product Owner provides right-time functional and business clarifications. The Scrum Master coaches, facilitates and serves the team and the organization.

The single team is a Scrum Team that delivers usable product functions that provide start-to-finish user value to the people using the product. The team is what is typically called a 'feature team'.

When adopting Scrum with a single team, the biggest challenge is to have all development skills in the team because in traditional organizations they are often scattered across different silo departments. But it is a must to get completely to Done within the Sprints. If that problem is overcome, the Sprint Review is fully transparent as an Increment holds no undone work, an important prerequisite to make the empirical approach of Scrum work. The team uses the Sprint Retrospective to improve itself.

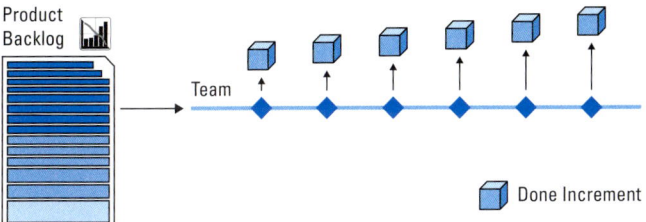

Figure 3.3 Single-team Scrum

3.8.2 Multi-team Scrum

For larger products, or when looking for faster results, the need may arise to maintain a product with more people than can conveniently work as one team. In such instances the need to work with multiple teams surfaces.

The multiple teams work on the product. They pull work from the same Product Backlog. The collective system has one Product Owner, with development organized in multiple teams (of Developers) and the support of one or more Scrum Masters. There are as many Sprint Backlogs as there are teams. Each individual team self-manages via a Daily Scrum.

The need for complete transparency over the integrity and usability of the total product at the Sprint Review remains. A product Increment cannot have undone, hidden work left. As the multiple teams are jointly building the same product, only fully *integrated* Increments assure the transparency and releasability needed.

The multiple teams self-organize within the boundaries of Scrum. When working in a construct of Multi-team Scrum, i.e. several teams creating and sustaining the same product, the teams still minimally self-manage, deciding who will do what work at what point in time without external interference. To optimize for the purpose of creating integrated Increments

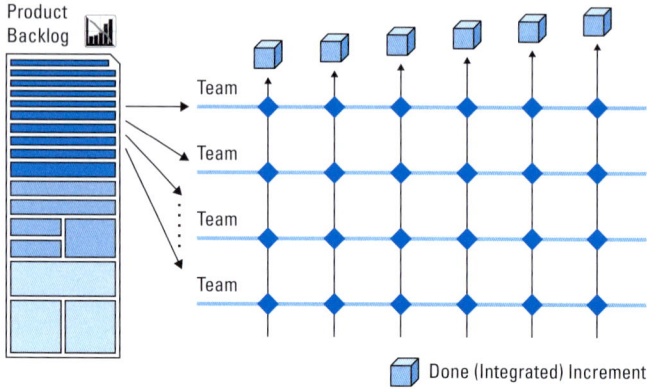

Figure 3.4 Multi-team Scrum

no later than by the end of a Sprint, they can demonstrate their self-designing capability by changing the teams' composition within the system.

Regular communication across the teams is required, throughout the Sprint, to align the different work plans against the objective of creating an integrated Increment. The teams extend the principle and purpose of the Daily Scrum to a cross-team level and organize *Scrum-of-Scrums* events.

In order to keep the whole optimized first, the Scrum-of-Scrums happens before the individual Daily Scrums. The most appropriate representatives of the teams gather to exchange development information, primarily focusing on the state of integration of the product and other cross-team dependencies. Subsequently, each individual team can safely re-plan and adjust its individual Sprint Backlog within the bigger multi-team ecosystem. As a result, the multiple teams optimize their joint progress while preserving integration of the whole. The technically sound Increments can be released if they comply with what is defined as Done, not hindered by open, unknown development work that is still to be performed.

The multiple teams work against the same quality criteria for the product expressed in the shared definition of Done. The multiple teams might find it easier to work on the same Sprint length to reduce the complexity of planning, integrating, releasing and reviewing the work. Additional work to keep their work integrated and healthy will be foreseen in their individual Sprint Backlogs.

In order to work on different Sprint lengths, a clear agreement and policies are crucial to assure all work is kept integrated continuously. A *green tree policy* is needed that takes precedence at all times. If anything breaks the whole, somewhere, sometime, that needs to be fixed first, indefinitely. As a result, each individual team or each combination of teams can (potentially independently) derive a releasable Increment from the shared codebase. The impact and consequences on infrastructure and architecture are not to be underestimated. Shared Sprint Reviews still make a lot of sense, though, to preserve functional and strategic alignment.

To deliver product Increments that provide start-to-finish user value, the combination of multiple teams in 'Multi-team Scrum' is a 'feature system'. Regardless of the composition of the individual teams (feature teams or otherwise), they collectively deliver integrated Increments of product, no later than by the end of a Sprint. All accountabilities defined by Scrum are fulfilled. The whole of the system is recognizably ... Scrum.

3.8.3 Multi-product Scrum

Depending on the functional or technical interdependency of multiple products, there may be a need for the work on the different products to be aligned and synchronized.

Each product has a Product Owner. For each product a Product Backlog exists with one or multiple teams to create, deliver and sustain it. Each product is maintained by a 'Single-team Scrum' or a 'Multi-team Scrum' instance.

From the accountabilities of Scrum, it is clear that alignment and synchronization primarily happen at the level of the Product Backlogs through the respective Product Owners. Individual Product Backlogs are additionally ordered upon optimization of the product line, the product suite, the program or the portfolio. The Product Owners incrementally manage their Product Backlogs on the basis of shared planning and progress information. If needed, a 'Backlog of Products' is maintained.

Technical and development dependencies across the different products are handled inner-Sprint by the different teams of Developers in a networked, non-hierarchical spirit. Communities of practice might emerge to unite people from different products and different teams around specific skill sets or expertise.

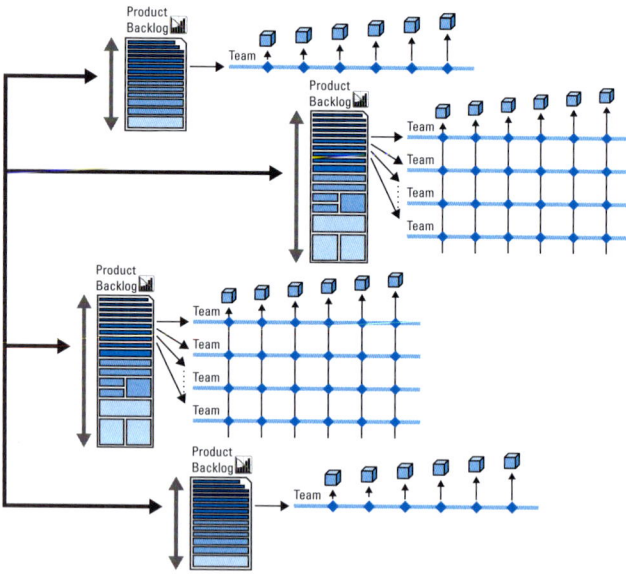

Figure 3.5 Multi-product Scrum

> Many more scaling problems, and therefore scenarios, exist. There is not one silver bullet solution. Scrum promotes bottom-up thinking with top-down support to discover and emerge what works best for you, your organization and your context.

4 The Future State of Scrum

Scrum emerged in the 1990s when pioneers like Ken Schwaber and Jeff Sutherland critically analyzed and reflected on practices that, at that time, were considered as common in software development and assessed them upon their own professional experience, successful product development strategies and process control theory. The sum of their experiential findings was formally presented as Scrum to the public in 1995 [Schwaber, 1995] [Sutherland, 1995]. Scrum as we know it today was subsequently shaped through the work of Ken Schwaber and Jeff Sutherland with a group of patterns people [Beedle, et.al., 1998]. In the years that have passed since the publication of the *'Manifesto for Agile Software Development'* [Beck, et.al., 2001] in 2001, Scrum became the most applied Agile framework worldwide. In 2010 the first version of the Scrum Guide was published, with updates in 2011, 2013, 2016, 2017 and 2020 [Verheyen, 2023].

Scrum has remained a light and simple way to organize complex work and address complex challenges. The unique combination of its clear definition and its low-prescriptive nature are paramount to its success, now and in the foreseeable future. Scrum, as a defined management framework, remains open as it can wrap various practices. It will render existing practices superfluous and reveal the need for new development, product management, quality, people and organizational practices. When applied well, they don't change Scrum.

Challenging the status quo of the industrial paradigm has already induced many advancements and has helped many organizations make the shift from predictive to empirical management. In many organizations the understanding has been restored that their work is actually a creative and complex activity performed by people, not robots. Many organizations now focus on products and services rather than temporary project constructs.

For many people worldwide, Scrum has become a proven solution. Despite the great results and the continued gorilla position of Scrum, there is room for improvement. There is a need to take it further. There is a better way. There must be.

There is a myriad of tactics, possibilities to play Scrum, and a myriad of practices that can be wrapped by Scrum. The results and outcome of the work managed with Scrum are influenced by many factors. The co-location of people influences it. The engagement, energy, dedication and joy of the people-players influence it. The level of self-organization influences it. The fact whether people have to multi-task influences it. The availability and access to tools, platforms and systems influence it. The willingness of people to see the cross-functional composition of teams as an opportunity to cross-fertilize and acquire new skills influences it.

Although it is worthwhile to take a closer look at each and every factor, one hugely crucial aspect is cross-functional thinking and acting beyond the walls of the development departments. Consider adopting Scrum to capitalize on business opportunities that benefit the enterprise, and the impact on the enterprise. Focus on product as it is the vehicle to deliver value. Remember that 'product' defines the scope of your Scrum and that 'product' can be a tangible or intangible product, service, device or experience.

From having implemented Scrum for the 'how' of work, shifting focus more to 'what' is to be done is more helpful than to keep merely optimizing the way that a product is being developed. *What is the point of increasing performance and producing more if you are heading in the wrong direction and the increased output is not what consumers actually require or appreciate?* Start discovering the power of the possible product rather than being restricted by the predicted product. It is part of shifting from volume to value.

See section 4.1 for more about "The Power of the Possible Product".

More than being about process and techniques, moving from the old, industrial paradigm to the new, Agile paradigm is about an organizational upgrade. The common enthusiasm in teams that arises from doing Scrum is unlikely to be sufficient for a much-needed system update and upgrade of organizational structures and constructs. It is unlikely to be sufficient to systematically re-organize around Scrum, including the way that leadership is organized. For a lasting effect of the adoption of Scrum, the support, facilitation and adoption of Scrum upstream is needed.

See section 4.2 for more about "The Upstream Adoption of Scrum".

■ 4.1 THE POWER OF THE POSSIBLE PRODUCT

The value that products bring can be greatly increased if we use Scrum to focus more on 'what' is being done, rather than just 'how' the work is being done; the capabilities, features, solutions and functions envisioned. It is a shift from (more) output to (better) outcomes, impact. Value is a very different driver than volume is.

In turbulent enterprise, business and market circumstances the predictability, certainty and stability of business requirements and functional expectations is low. Improved and active collaboration with business owners and product managers cannot be skipped in the continual journey of optimizing for value. These people must be actively involved to overcome the unavoidable absence of full agreement over features and requirements upfront. And more than ever these product people will benefit from the flexibility that Scrum offers to capitalize on unforeseen opportunities and have the best possible product out there at the right time. What is appreciated today might not be what people are looking for tomorrow.

With Scrum, organizations can finally stop trying to predict the inherently unpredictable and deal with answers, solutions and ideas that emerge while maintaining and evolving a product that is already in production. Scrum renders the question of whether issues were thought of upfront as irrelevant. Requirements as the input for the product delivery ecosystem are no longer expected to be complete, final and exhaustive. Scrum helps in accepting and embracing the fact that the final agreement on the 'what' of the product only gets resolved *while* creating it. Optimizing for value requires validating internal decisions frequently through actual usage in the marketplace. Scrum opens the door for frequent functional releases to ensure regular progress and learning and to stop merely accumulating (invalidated) assumptions as would happen in sequential open loop systems. When connection to the marketplace is tight, real user feedback can be incorporated through the living artifact that Product Backlog is.

In Scrum, the Product Owner is accountable for deciding what to do (next). The Product Owner envisions the next Product Goal or the next release or version of the product for the marketplace. The mandate of the Product Owner influences the level of agility an organization achieves with Scrum. On top of that mandate, a Product Owner needs a close connection to all related product management domains: marketing, communication, sales, legal, research, finance, support, etc. It is essential to have multi-disciplined collaboration across organizational walls. Involving different product management skills leverages the use of Scrum for *enterprise* agility. In a globalizing world of ever-increasing internal and external unpredictability, adopting a mindset of empiricism and adaptiveness is beneficial to entire organizations.

Employing Scrum is not about renaming or slightly reworking old techniques that are rooted in the industrial paradigm. Product Backlog is not the new name for the traditional requirements list or predictive plan. Product Owner is not the new name for the requirements analyst gathering requirements and throwing them over the wall to the programmers. Nor does it suffice to act as proxies without a mandate, stakeholder backing, budget responsibility and real user representation.

The role of Product Owner as envisioned by Scrum did not exist in the industrial paradigm. Product Owner is a living example of cross-functional thinking. The professional life of a Product Owner revolves around the product, not a department or a title. The Product Owner ultimately acts as the Product-CEO, thereby guided, coached and facilitated by a Scrum Master. Management and executive representatives act as investors and sponsors having control from the boundaries, like from attending the Sprint Reviews. Scrum becomes the beating heart of organization-wide agility in generating a regular flow of improvements, learnings and various other sources of information that help in optimizing for value; value to the stakeholders, value to the users and consumers of the products and services, value to the people creating and maintaining them, value to communities, society and the environment.

Once 'product' becomes front and center in Scrum and becomes the single focus for the teams dedicated to maintaining and evolving them, more and different skills are gathered around the product, permanently, further cutting through silos and layers of the organization. A *Product Hub* emerges, a value-driven organization-within-the-organization.

Ultimately, an enterprise, its networked Product Hubs and its markets become a self-balancing continuum, with players contributing across barriers, domains, skills and functions. Organizations can discover, experiment and deliver on opportunities from an end-to-end perspective in the fastest possible way with Scrum.

■ 4.2 THE UPSTREAM ADOPTION OF SCRUM

When adopting Scrum, the broader organization is impacted. Period. There is no way to deeply adopt Scrum without disruptions rippling through the complete organization.

Issues that go beyond the Scrum Teams will pop up and need to be taken care of in order to gain the full benefit of Scrum: funding, product management, HR, support, sales, compliance and regulations, quality assurance. Organizational opportunities and improvement areas to better facilitate the Scrum Teams and thereby improve the complete space of product delivery are discovered through the application of Scrum.

Organizations wanting to use Scrum to effectively progress on their journey of agility should be aware that this will not be achieved by implementing Scrum just for the sake of it. Scrum cannot be the purpose of Scrum. Scrum has the potential to increase agility at an organizational or enterprise level. Scrum is not designed to be the new IT process, but rather is a framework of rules, principles and values to enable organizations to capitalize on the unforeseeable. Scrum enables fast adaptation to go from following to leading the market and provide competitive advantage (again).

A vast majority of organizations unfortunately act as if they still reside in the land of *Mediocristan*. The characteristics for that 'state' of society, as described by Nassim Nicholas Taleb in his book '*The Black Swan*' [Taleb, 2007], are that success has a direct relationship to the hours or effort spent on non-scalable, repetitive work. Taleb describes how Mediocristan has become an illusion of the past. It has been replaced by *Extremistan*, where success depends on the 'production' of ideas and the elaboration of unpredicted singularities. Scrum has what it takes to beam up the inhabitants of Mediocristan to Extremistan, so they become at least 'a' player in Extremistan, and potentially even a leader, a giant. Scrum can be the engine for adapting so fast that it's up to their competitors to respond to the change that an organization causes. Leading the game comes within reach, outplaying the rest of the field, being the giant.

But it starts with accepting, or rather embracing, that we operate in a market state of Extremistan. It starts with accepting, or rather provoking, that our organizations must change not to fade, even without the realization that the fourth Scrum Wave coincides with entering the Tornado phase of Agile with Scrum as the gorilla method. The industrial fundaments on which a majority of them are constructed have been invalidated anyhow. *Our iceberg is melting*, is the metaphor in the tale of Holger Rathgeber and change expert John P. Kotter [Kotter & Rathgeber, 2006]. Ignoring or belittling the huge shift towards complexity is an important cause of a lack of upstream adoption for Scrum. And it seriously limits the benefits realized by playing the game of Scrum. It undermines your future leadership, and even survival.

In larger organizations, Scrum Teams and Scrum Masters have limited or no control over the bureaucratic obligations related to the delivery and the release of products. Often teams have to operate on the basis of compliancy expectations and ceremonial rules that were put in place as part of the industrial paradigm. They are being maintained beyond the actual experience and lack of success of building products in today's world. In many cases these procedures, and therefore their organizations, have grown out of step with the rapid evolutions that are so typical for today's markets, external circumstances and internal organizational evolutions.

Nevertheless, the experience with Scrum in a vast majority of organizations is excellent and lives up to a sense of common sense. In my experience, Scrum often restores the 'common' to the 'sense'. The inhabitants of the house of Scrum appreciate Scrum because it thrives on and creates much enthusiasm. No surprise that this is exactly why *downstream adoption* is generally huge, although often only as long as management, leadership and traditionalists can be kept out.

One would expect that proven results, improved figures and increased delivery of value would lead to more upstream interest and supported adoption of the real thing. My experience contradicts this expectation.

Your organization deserves active and explicit upstream support and promotion of Scrum. Think about operational IT management, sales divisions, delivery managers, product management departments and hierarchical CxO management.

It takes a sense of urgency, whilst acknowledging that there indeed *is* urgency. It starts by accepting the inconvenient truth that comfort, certainty and control do not come from traditional predictions and plans. Comfort comes from reality, from proven experience, observable working results and empirical data instead of static and gamed reports. The traditional formalisms of the industrial paradigm have not resulted in improved execution and increased value. Requirements turn out not to be required, markets change, unexpected expectations appear, priorities shift. Complex problems are dynamic, not static. They change shape as they get tackled.

Upstream adoption is a matter of 'management'. The goal of a lasting Scrum transformation is to involve managers in the game through a structured, iterative-incremental approach of the needed organizational upgrade. The goal for managers is to re-invent themselves, their role and their work. Such an approach thrives upon urgency for improvement, meanwhile capitalizing on the downstream enthusiasm that exists over Scrum. Such an upgrade is not achieved in a mass-production or cascaded waterfall way. A typical waterfall transition starts with adopting Scrum and resolving the 'problem' of cross-functional teams first. This often reveals a lack of engineering facilities and support, so that domain is tackled next. After addressing the engineering area, an enterprise might want to increase business involvement. And so on. Depending on the size of the enterprise, it can easily take one to three years per area. In the end, it is a series of linearly sequenced open-loop systems, offering no chances of success in high complexity. In the meantime, no more than an illusion of agility is created. After several years the organization realizes that its agility has not been substantially increased. This reality leads to an experience of deflation, a deflation by reality.

An organizational transformation based on Scrum addresses changes in enterprise domains *concurrently*, producing Increments of change. A transformation changes how an organization works, rather than adding work and meetings on top of what people already do. Adopting Scrum can be expected to simplify how work is done, maximize the work not done, engage people. A genuine transformation has no direction: it is bottom-up, top-down, left-right, right-left, inside-out, outside-in. At the same time. An organizational upgrade, via an Agile transformation or otherwise, should be based on the premise that people are naturally Agile, that they have the natural ability to adapt. The process of Scrum follows people in the sense that it builds on their natural ability to adapt. Finally, structure should follow this process (not the other way around) that follows people. *Adapt the organization to Scrum, not the other way around.*

Cross-functional change is implemented in small steps in parallel in several domains while the overall effects of the incremental steps are measured. The regular inspections of enterprise or product-level measurements form the base for informed decisions on the next steps and practices in the various domains. Close the feedback loop. Measurements should mirror an organization's ability to deliver value. These measurements are not targets but pointers to improvement areas; re-humanization, education, dedicated teams, a shared (visual) workspace, tools, standards. Inspection without adaptation is pointless.

The vertical silo-like departments become dimmed. Barriers get removed. Communities emerge. Authority moves down the line. Accountability grows. Organizational structures and processes re-emerge. Product Hubs come into existence. Leadership becomes a distributed quality. Agility occurs and becomes an inherent quality of the organization.

And remember, agility can't be planned, dictated or copied, as agility is unique and has no end-state.

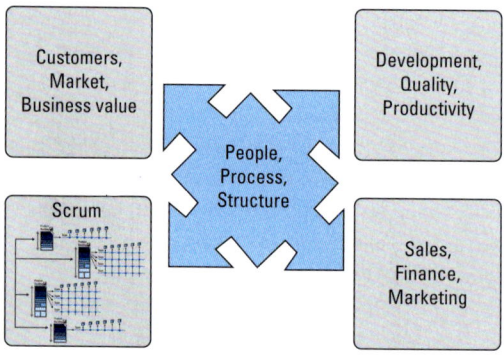

Figure 4.1 Enterprise Scrum Transformation

The future state of Scrum will no longer be called 'Scrum'. What we now call Scrum will have become the norm, and we will have re-organized around it while humanizing our workplace.

Annex A: Scrum Glossary

Burn-down Chart: a chart showing the decrease of remaining work against time.

Burn-up Chart: a chart showing the increase of a parameter, like value, against time.

Daily Scrum: a daily event, time-boxed to 15 minutes or less, to re-plan the development work during a Sprint. The event serves to share the daily progress, plan the work for the next 24 hours and update Sprint Backlog accordingly.

Definition of Done: the set of expectations on quality that a product Increment must exhibit to make it releasable, meaning fit for a release to the product's consumers.

Developers (team of): the people accountable for all evolutionary development work needed to create a releasable Increment no later than by the end of a Sprint. *Formerly known as 'Development Team'.*

Development standards: the set of standards and practices that are identified as needed to create releasable Increments of product no later than by the end of a Sprint.

Emergence: the process of the coming into existence or prominence of unforeseen facts or knowledge of a fact, a previously unknown fact, or knowledge of a fact becoming visible unexpectedly.

Empiricism: the process control type in which decisions are based on observed results, experience and experimentation. Empiricism implements regular inspections and adaptations requiring and creating transparency. *Also referred to as 'empirical process control'.*

Forecast: the anticipation of a future trend based on observations of the past, like the selection of Product Backlog deemed deliverable in the current Sprint or in future Sprints for future Product Backlog.

Impediment: any hindrance or obstacle that is blocking or slowing down the development work and cannot be solved through the self-organization of a team. Raised no later than at the Daily Scrum, the Scrum Master is accountable for its removal.

Increment: a candidate of releasable work that adds to and changes previously created Increments and – as a whole – form a product.

Product: A tangible or non-tangible good, device, service or experience providing value to identified consumers. *Defines the span of Product Owner, Product Backlog and Increment.*

Product Backlog: an ordered, evolving list of all work deemed potentially valuable to create, deliver, maintain and sustain a product by the Product Owner.

Product Backlog refinement: the recurring activity in a Sprint through which granularity is added to future Product Backlog.

Product Owner: the person accountable for optimizing the value a product delivers, primarily by managing and expressing all product expectations and ideas in a Product Backlog.

Scrum (n): an empirical framework to manage complex product development (1); an empirical framework for addressing complex challenges (2); an empirical framework that enables people to derive value from complex challenges (3).

Scrum Master: the person accountable for fostering an environment of Scrum by guiding, coaching, teaching and advising one or more Scrum Teams and their environment in understanding and employing Scrum.

Scrum Team: the combined accountabilities of Product Owner, (team of) Developers and Scrum Master.

Scrum Values: a set of five fundamental values and qualities underpinning the Scrum framework: commitment, focus, openness, respect and courage.

Self-design: the expression of self-organization where only the team decides what skills are, or are not, needed and present within the team.

Self-management: the minimal expression of self-organization in Scrum, holding that only the team decides how to perform the work within a Sprint.

Self-organization: the process of people forming organized groups around problems or challenges without external work plans or instructions being imposed on them.

Sprint: an event that serves as a container for the other Scrum events, time-boxed to four weeks or less. The event serves getting a sufficient amount of work done, while ensuring timely inspection, reflection and adaptation at a product, strategic and process level. *The contained Scrum events are Sprint Planning, Daily Scrum, Sprint Review and Sprint Retrospective.*

Sprint Backlog: an evolving plan of all work deemed necessary to realize a Sprint's goal.

Sprint Goal: a concise statement expressing the overarching purpose of a Sprint.

Sprint length: time-box of a Sprint, which is four weeks or less.

Sprint Planning: an event marking the start of a Sprint, time-boxed to eight hours or less. The event serves for the Scrum Team to inspect the Product Backlog considered most valuable at that time and design a selection from it, the forecast, into an initial Sprint Backlog with a Sprint Goal.

Sprint Retrospective: an event marking the closing of a Sprint, time-boxed to three hours or less. The event serves for the Scrum Team to inspect the Sprint that is ending and consider the way of working for the next Sprint.

Sprint Review: an event marking the closing of the development of a Sprint, time-boxed to four hours or less. The event serves for the Scrum Team and the product's stakeholders to inspect the Increment(s), the overall progress and strategic changes in order to allow the Product Owner to update the Product Backlog so that it best reflects the current priorities.

Stakeholder: a person external to the Scrum Team with a specific interest in, or knowledge of, a product that is required for the further evolution of the product.

Team: a cross-functional collective of people committed to the shared purpose of creating valuable Increments of product.

Time-box: a container in time of a maximum duration, potentially a fixed duration. *In Scrum all events have a maximum duration, except for the Sprint itself which has a fixed duration.*

Velocity: popular indication of the average amount of Product Backlog turned into an Increment of releasable product during a Sprint by a specific (composition of a) team.

Annex B: Scrum Reference Card

Scrum sets no more than minimal boundaries to elevate self-organization with frequent reminders for all people-players to enact empiricism, i.e. adapt upon inspections (of reality). All rules, principles and values of the framework serve this purpose.

The time-boxes set a minimal frequency for the specific inspection and adaptation process that happens at the various events. Scrum assures that the art of empiricism is performed no later than at the time of its events.

The Scrum artifacts contain the information to be inspected and adapted.

The following reference card describes the time-boxes and purpose of all events in terms of the main input ("Inspection") and expected outcome ("Adaptation") of every event, as well as who minimally must attend each event to assure all insights are represented:

Event	Inspection	Adaptation	Attendants	Time-box
Sprint Planning	• Product Backlog (Past performance) (Availabilities) (Retrospective commitments) (Definition of Done)	• Sprint Backlog (Forecast+ Plan+ Sprint Goal)	Scrum Team	Max 8 hours
Daily Scrum	• Sprint Progress (toward the Sprint Goal)	• Sprint Backlog (Plan)	(team of) Developers	Max 15 minutes
Sprint Review	• Product Increment • Product Backlog (& progress Toward the Product Goal) • Market & business conditions	• Product Backlog	Scrum Team Stakeholders (Users)	Max 4 hours
Sprint Retrospective	• Current Sprint (Value and definition of Done) (Team and collaboration) (Technology and development)	• Next Sprint (Way of working) (Actionable improvements) (Experiments)	Scrum Team	Max 3 hours
Sprint				4 weeks or less

Annex C: References

Adkins, L. (2010). *Coaching Agile Teams, A Companion for ScrumMasters, Agile Coaches, and Project Managers in Transition.* Addison-Wesley.

Beck, K. (2000). *Extreme Programming Explained – Embrace Change.* Addison-Wesley.

Beck, K., Beedle, M., v. Bennekum, A., Cockburn, A., Cunningham, W., Fowler, M., Grenning, J., Highsmith, J., Hunt, A., Jeffries, R., Kern, J., Marick, B., Martin, R. C., Mellor, S., Schwaber, K., Sutherland, J., Thomas, D. (February 2001). *Manifesto for Agile Software Development.* http://agilemanifesto.org/

Beck, K., Fowler, M. (2001). *Planning Extreme Programming.* Addison-Wesley.

Beedle, M., Devos, M., Schwaber, K., Sharon, Y., Sutherland, J. (December 1998). *SCRUM: An extension pattern language for hyperproductive software development.*

Benefield, G. (2008). *Rolling Out Agile at a Large Enterprise.* HICSS'41 (Hawaii International Conference on Software Systems).

Cockburn, A. (2002). *Agile Software Development.* Addison-Wesley.

DeGrace, P., Hulet Stahl, L. (1990). *Wicked Problems, Righteous Solutions.* Prentice Hall.

Giudice, D. L. (November 2011). *Global Agile Software Application Development Online Survey.* Forrester Research.

Hammond, J., West, D. (October 2009). *Agile Application Lifecycle Management.* Forrester Research.

Highsmith, J. (2023). *Wild West to Agile (Adventures in Software Development Evolution and Revolution).* Pearson Education, Inc.

Kotter, J., Rathgeber, H. (2006). *Our Iceberg Is Melting, Changing and Succeeding Under Any Conditions.* MacMillan.

Larman, C. (2004). *Agile & Iterative Development, A Manager's Guide.* Addison-Wesley.

Larman, C., Vodde, B. (2009). *Lean Primer.* http://www.leanprimer.com

Moore, G. (1999). *Crossing the Chasm, Marketing and Selling Technology Products to Mainstream Customers (second edition).* Wiley.

Pink, D. (2009). *Drive: The Surprising Truth About What Motivates Us.* Riverhead Books.

Rock, D. (2008). *SCARF: a brain-based model for collaborating with and influencing others.* NeuroLeadership Journal.

Schwaber, K. (October 1995). *SCRUM Software Development Process.*

Schwaber, K., Beedle, M. (2001). *Agile Software Development with Scrum.* Prentice Hall.

Schwaber, K., Sutherland, J. (November 2020). *The Scrum Guide.* http://www.scrumguides.org.

Standish Group (2002). Keynote on Feature Usage in a Typical System at XP2002 Congress by Jim Johnson, Chairman of the Standish Group. Results from a study of 2000 projects at 1000 companies.

Standish Group (2011). *Chaos Manifesto (The Laws of Chaos and the Chaos 100 Best PM Practices).* The Standish Group International.

Standish Group (2013). *Chaos Manifesto 2013: Think big, act small.* Standish Group.

Sutherland, J. (1995) OOPSLA '95 - Business Object Design and Implementation Workshop. http://www.jeffsutherland.org/oopsla/schwaber.html

Sutherland, J. (October 2011). *Takeuchi and Nonaka: The Roots of Scrum.* http://scrum.jeffsutherland.com/2011/10/takeuchi-and-nonaka-roots-of-scrum.html

Taleb, N. N. (2007). *The Black Swan - The Impact of the Highly Improbable*. Random House.

Takeuchi, H., Nonaka, I. (January-February 1986). *The New New Product Development Game*. Harvard Business Review.

Verheyen, G. (December 2011). *The Blending Philosophies of Lean and Agile*. Scrum.org (https://www.scrum.org/resources/blending-philosophies-lean-and-agile).

Verheyen, G., Arooni, A. (December 2012). *ING, Capturing Agility via Scrum at a large Dutch bank*. Scrum.org (https://www.scrum.org/resources/ing-capturing-agility-scrum-large-dutch-bank).

Verheyen, G. (2020). *97 Things Every Scrum Practitioner Should Know*. O'Reilly Media.

Verheyen, G. (March 2019-May 2022). *The illusion of agility (What most 'Agile transformations' deliver)*. Ullizee-Inc (https://guntherverheyen.com/wp-content/uploads/2022/05/The-Illusion-of-Agility-Paper.pdf).

Verheyen, G. (December 2020-September 2023). *Scrum: A Brief History of a Long-Lived Hype*. Ullizee-Inc (https://guntherverheyen.com/wp-content/uploads/2023/09/Scrum-A-Brief-History-of-a-Long-Lived-Hype-v1.3-Sep-2023-Paper.pdf).

VersionOne (2011). *State of Agile Survey. 6th Annual*. VersionOne Inc.

VersionOne (2013). *7th Annual State of Agile Development Survey*. VersionOne Inc.

Wiefels, P. (2002). *The Chasm Companion. A Fieldbook to Crossing the Chasm and Inside the Tornado*. Wiley.

About the Author

Gunther Verheyen calls himself an independent Scrum Caretaker on a journey of humanizing the workplace with Scrum. He thinks, reflects, wonders and wanders. He teaches, assists, serves, advises and suggests. He works with teams, individuals and executives. He facilitates learning and unlearning. He has been employing Scrum since 2003, has published two best-selling books about Scrum and has partnered with Ken Schwaber, co-creator of Scrum.

Gunther ventured into IT and software development after graduating as an Industrial Engineer in electronics in 1992.

His Agile adventures started with eXtreme Programming wrapped in Scrum in 2003. Until 2010 he gained experience with Scrum with various teams in various organizations and diverse domains. He then became the inspiring force behind some large-scale enterprise transformations. In 2011 he acquired his license as a Professional Scrum Trainer for Scrum.org.

Gunther left consulting in 2013 to establish Ullizee-Inc and partner exclusively with Ken Schwaber, co-creator of Scrum. He managed the "Professional Scrum" series of Scrum.org and shepherded its global network of Professional Scrum Trainers. He co-created Agility Path, EBM (Evidence-Based Management) and the Nexus framework for Scaled Professional Scrum.

Since 2016 Gunther is continuing his journey to humanize the workplace with Scrum as an independent Scrum Caretaker; a connector, teacher, writer, speaker. He helps organizations re-imagine their Scrum and re-organize around it while creating a more humane and therefore more productive workplace.

Gunther published the book '*Scrum – A Pocket Guide*' in 2013, which was recommended by Ken Schwaber as "the best description of Scrum currently available". A second edition was published in 2019, a third edition in 2021 and the current, fourth edition in 2024. In 2020 Gunther published the book '*97 Things Every Scrum Practitioner Should Know*' with essays from field experts across the world. Several translations of his work are available.

When not traveling to humanize the workplace with Scrum, Gunther lives and works in Antwerp (Belgium). He delivers his Scrum Services through Ullizee-Inc. More at https://guntherverheyen.com/.

"Scrum is free. The Scrum framework is immutable. While implementing only parts of Scrum is possible, the result is not Scrum. Scrum exists only in its entirety and functions well as a container for other techniques, methodologies, and practices."

(Ken Schwaber, Jeff Sutherland, The Scrum Guide)

Index

A

adaptiveness 31
adaptive problems 74
Adkins, Lyssa 69
Agile and Lean 31, 34
Agile, definition 21
Agile Development 91
Agile Manifesto 20
Agile movement 43
Agile paradigm 17
agility 28, 112

B

Bowling Alley 43
burn-down chart 59
burn-up chart 60

C

change 23
Chaos reports (Standish Group) 16
Chasm 44
closed loop system 74
Collective (Code) Ownership 91
commitment, definition 78
complexity 72
conflicts 69
continuous improvement 33, 37
Continuous Integration 91
cost 63
courage 81
cultural change 29

D

Daily Scrum 56, 75, 86
Daily Stand-up 87
definition of Done 54, 64, 91
desirement 62
Developer 54
Done Increments 54

E

emergence 24
Empirical process control 72
Empiricism 49

extreme development 91
eXtreme Programming 87, 91

G
gorilla 44
Grenning, James 90

H
House of Scrum 39

I
impediment 69
Increment 53
industrial paradigm 16, 78
INVEST (Independent, Negotiable, Valuable, Estimable, Sized appropriately, Testable) 89
iterative-incremental process 23

K
Kaizen 32
Kotter, John P. 109

L
Lean 31, 33, 34

M
Manifesto for Agile Software Development 20, 95
Moore, Geoffrey 43

N
Nonaka, Ikujiro 40

O
open loop system 73
openness 80

P
Pair Development 92
Pair Programming 91, 92
Pink, Daniel 68
Planning Poker 90
predictive plan 73
Product Backlog 53, 60, 64, 92
Product Backlog refinement 87
Product Goal 57, 59, 61, 85
Product Hub 107
Product Owner 52, 57, 61, 67, 96, 99, 106

R
Rathgeber, Holger 109
Refectoring 91
Release Burn-down chart 85
respect for people 38, 80
risk 26

S
Schwaber, Ken 41, 103
Scrum 40, 95
    best practices 83
    future state 103
    good tactics 84
    House of 39
    multi-product 99
    Multi-team 97

scale of 46, 95
Single-team 96
upstream adoption 108
values 77
Scrum Board 60, 85
Scrum Game Board 52, 66
Scrum Guide 8, 103
Scrum Master 54, 66, 70, 96, 109
Scrum-of-Scrums 98
Scrum process for software development 43
Scrum Reference Card 119
Scrum Team 52, 56, 108
Scrum Vitals 84
self-organization 41, 49, 66
self-organizing team 41, 70
shared workspace 70
Sprint 53, 54, 56, 75
Sprint length 93
Sprint Planning 56
Sprint Retrospective 57
Sprint Review 57
stakeholders 57
State of Agile Development (VersionOne), survey 46
Sutherland, Jeff 41, 103

T

Takeuchi, Hirotaka 40
Taleb, Nassim Nicholas 108
Taylor, Frederick 15
Technology Adoption Life Cycle (TALC) 43
Test-driven Development 91
time-boxed iteration 25, 55
Total Cost of Ownership (TCO) 27
Toyota Production System 43
transparency 49, 64, 74, 80, 89, 91

U

User Story 89

V

value 26, 53, 60, 63, 105
Value Ratio 33
Value Stream Mapping 33
Velocity 58
visualizing progress 84

W

Wake, Bill 89
waste 33
  avoiding 33
waterfall approach 20, 45
WIP (Work in Process) 36, 92

Y

YAGNI (You Ain't Gonna Need It) 79